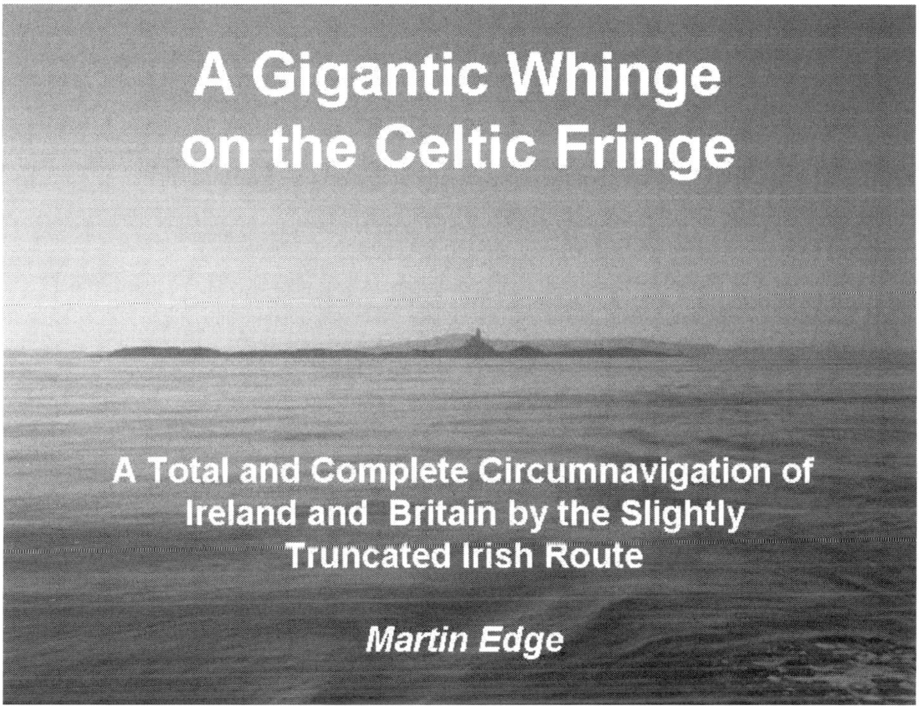

A Gigantic Whinge on the Celtic Fringe

A Total and Complete Circumnavigation of Ireland and Britain by the Slightly Truncated Irish Route

Martin Edge

This rubbish is dedicated to my uncle, John Edge, a Yachtmaster and sailor of 70 years experience, who read previous accounts of my voyages and actually claimed to enjoy them.

A Gigantic Whinge
on the Celtic Fringe

A Total and Complete Circumnavigation of Ireland and Britain by the Slightly Truncated Irish Route

Zophiel's Cruise in 2011

Martin Edge

First Print Edition 2014
Published in Great Britain 2011 by Martin Edge
Copyright © Martin Edge 2011.

Martin Edge asserts the right under the Copyright, Designs and Patents Act 1988 to be identified as the author of this work. All rights reserved. No part of this publication may be reproduced in any material form (including photocopying or storing in any medium by electronic means and whether or not transiently or incidentally to some other use of this publication) without the written permission of the copyright holder except in accordance with the provisions of the Copyright, Design and Patents Act 1988 or under the terms of a licence issued by the Copyright Licensing Agency Ltd. This book is sold subject to the conditions that it shall not, by way of trade or otherwise, be lent, re-sold, hired out, or otherwise circulated without the author's prior consent in any form binding or cover other than that in which it is published and without a similar condition, including this condition, being imposed on the subsequent purchaser.

The full sets of colour pictures from this and other volumes of Zophiel's travels are available free at:

http://www.edge.me.uk

Table of Malcontents

	Page
Preface	
A Preliminary Whinge	5
Deliverance	9
Wild West	15
Cranium	25
Neck and Shoulder	33
Shoulder Arms	38
Into Ireland's Oxter	45
Belly Button and Legs	53
Behind Ireland's Knees	64
Round Ireland's Arse	72
The Front line of the Celtic Fringe	77
Ancestral Home	81
The Scouse Celts	88
On Mill Pond	101
Treading Water	110
Livery	115
Postscript	126

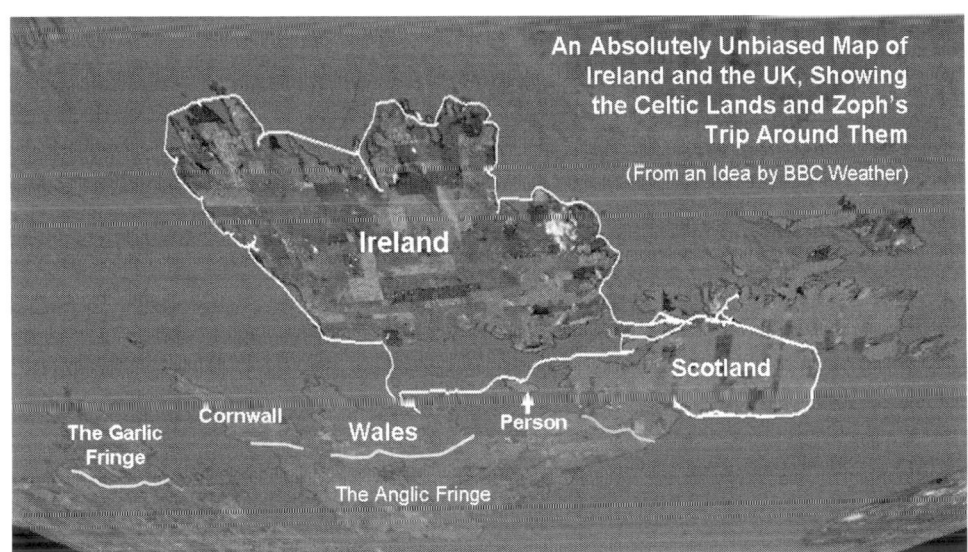

Preface

This is the holiday journal of a floating, ranting wimp. It is the tale of that wimp's progress round the seas of northern Europe.

In 2003 I bought a small and slightly scruffy yacht called *'Zophiel'*. Though rather small for long distance cruising, the cutter rigged Vancouver is a seaworthy heavyweight. The first one was designed for a couple of nutters who were emigrating from Canada to New Zealand and wanted to do it in a 27ft sailing boat. Other Vancouvers have crossed oceans and sailed round the world.

My ambitions are rather more modest. Actually that's not true. I'd love to join the ranks of the fearless ocean navigators and sail round the world. But, as I've already mentioned, I'm a bit of a wimp.

So over the past few years I've spent summers cruising around parts of northern Europe from Zophiel's base under the Forth Bridge near Edinburgh. Most of these journeys have been sailed solo but sometimes I've had a crew, particularly for the longer sea crossings. Again, I'm no Joshua Slocum.

'A Gigantic Whinge on the Celtic Fringe' is the third tale of these cruises. It describes my circumnavigation of Ireland in 2011.

Though I started out writing a straightforward description of the trip, the world is an extremely annoying place so, as usual, it ended up as an extended series of rants and ramblings. These are mostly about the condition of the lands of the UK and Ireland that are often, somewhat disparagingly, described as the 'Celtic Fringe'.

So I hope this account of a sailing trip, as well as being reasonably entertaining, will give some pause for thought about a few issues, even though it's just the ramblings of a holidaying wimp.

The Celtic Fringe Whinge is the follow-up to *"Floating Low to Lofoten"*, which describes Zophiel's 2008 cruise north along the coast of Norway to north of the Arctic Circle. *"Skagerrak and Back"*, which described Zophiel's 2007 North Sea circuit, was the first in the series. *"Bobbing to the Baltic"* is the tale of her trip in 2012 from Edinburgh to the Russian border with Finland and most of the way back.

Martin Edge
December 2011

A Preliminary Whinge

This year I decided to sail round Ireland. Most people say that the clockwise route is best, as you beat against the prevailing south-westerlies in the sheltered waters of the Irish Sea, running with the wind and constant ocean swell up the exposed Atlantic coast.

As usual I ended up going the wrong way by the perverse route, anticlockwise. There was a rationale. Going anticlockwise I had options when I reached the bottom of Ireland. I could return the easy way, up the Irish Sea. I could continue east and circumnavigate England via the wilds of the little frequented south coast and such remote and uncharted places as 'The Solent'. I could continue south across Biscay to places where, it is rumoured, the sun comes out and temperatures soar above 12 degrees.

In the event I took the wimpy option and came back up the Irish Sea. This allowed me to visit a lot of the bits of what is sometimes called the 'Celtic Fringe'. If you consider the south east of England to be the centre of something then the broadly speaking Celtic bits of the British Isles can be considered a 'fringe'. The west of Scotland, Ireland - the Republic and the North, Wales, Cornwall and Brittany all lie on the edge of the Atlantic. From the perspective of someone travelling on a road or rail network they are remote from the 'centre' and hence on the 'fringe'.

Once you start travelling independently by sea and are not constrained by ferry routes, you realise that the fragmented bits of this 'Celtic Fringe' are more or less contiguous. They form a connected whole.

This was what it was like for our ancestors, for whom the sea was not so much a barrier but the main highway, albeit a dangerous and fraught one. It was easier to travel long distances by sea than through the boggy, tangled undergrowth of most of England. The latter was an uninviting swamp on the fringe of the Celtic world. So whilst I was writing an account of a journey by sea I couldn't resist sounding off about the Celtic lands and some of the issues facing them.

Being something of a self-publicist I made a small study of how high profile solo sailors make names for themselves. In many cases the answer seems to be shameless exaggeration. Recently an Australian girl claimed to be the youngest solo circumnavigator of the world by nipping round the Southern Ocean and making a quick detour over the equator just into the northern hemisphere. A remarkable feat way beyond the wildest dreams of most of us, but not, strictly speaking, a circumnavigation.

Somewhat lesser mortals routinely set out to circumnavigate Britain. It is quite shocking how many of these, including some I met this year on my travels, not only cut inside most of the islands on their journey, but actually sail right through the middle of Britain down the Caledonian Canal.

These don't just include con artists like the bloke I saw motoring up the canal with his girlfriend as crew with the legend "Sailing Around Britain Single-Handed" emblazoned across his boat. When questioned he said, "Oh all that stuff to the north isn't really Britain". They also include very well known names like famously fearless sailor and professional crier-to-camera Ellen MacArthur.

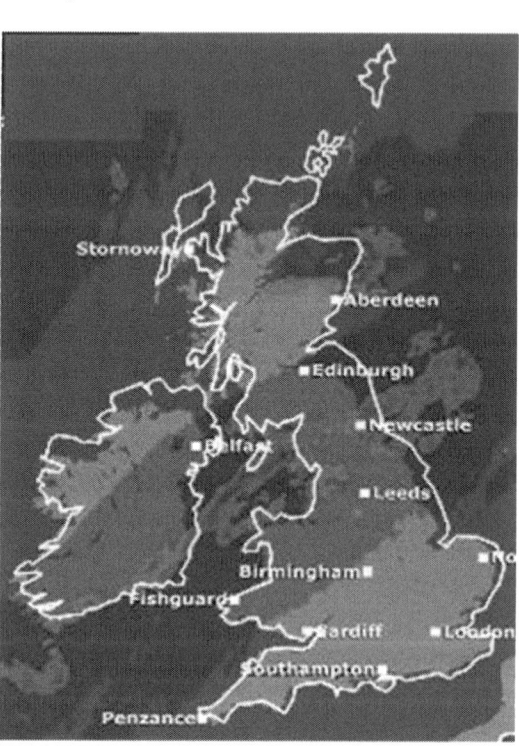

The outline is an objective map of the UK and Ireland seen from directly above the middle. Beneath is the weather map the BBC uses as propaganda to convince a generation that Scotland is half the size it actually is and that Shetland barely exists at all. I've merely applied the same sort of technique to my objective map of the Celtic bits

It is quite astonishing how many highly accomplished, driven sailors, with obsessive personal goals, are happy to cheat as soon as the weather turns nasty, yet still proclaim their success as circumnavigators.

They mostly get away with it for two reasons. Firstly, a generation has now grown up which is used to the BBC weather map of the UK. This curious creation has been produced to 'downsize' Scotland and increase the apparent size of the south of England, by tilting the country up so that the north of Scotland all but disappears in the distance. So a generation of English people now believes that Scotland is about half the size it actually is. Secondly, they do it for charity, so that all but the most churlish (me) let them off with it.

If you Google MacArthur's circumnavigation of Britain it's actually quite hard to disentangle her route from the strident statements about her astonishing bravery. But yes, she, like many others, insultingly cocked a snook at highlanders, pretended they didn't exist and happily sailed up the middle.

"Oh, I'd like to have sailed round the top via the Pentland Firth and Cape Wrath", some of them say "But it was difficult and the weather turned nasty and I was behind schedule, so I sailed round Britain by the slightly shorter, lowland route". To which I reply "I'd have liked to have sailed across the Southern Ocean and round Cape Horn, but it's difficult and the weather turned nasty so I stayed at home in bed, but I'll claim I did it anyway".

Of course if you want to do a total circumnavigation of Britain and are a properly driven pedant, like one would have thought MacArthur to be, you'd want to go round all the islands. If you did then the southern half, from Fort Bill southwards, round the Scillies, along the south coast, up the east and round to Inverness, is a minimum of about 1260 miles. The northern half, out of Inverness, round Muckle Flugga, St Kilda and the outer Hebrides (we'll let her off with Rockall, which remained disputed territory) and back to Fort Bill, is about 1000 miles.

One day I'm going to head from my base on the Forth, round the Pentland Firth and Cape Wrath, down to the Bristol Channel where I'll get the mast taken down. I'll head through the English canal system to the Thames then sail back up the east coast to the Forth. I will, of course, claim a circumnavigation of Britain and see whether there's any objections from sailors in the south of England.

But in 2011 I took a leaf out of Ellen MacArthur's book and lied through my teeth to try and get publicity. I'm even less principled than most, so I claimed a Total and Complete Circumnavigation of Ireland and Britain by the Slightly Truncated Irish Route.

Solpieter cheats by using a huge electric fan to blow her along

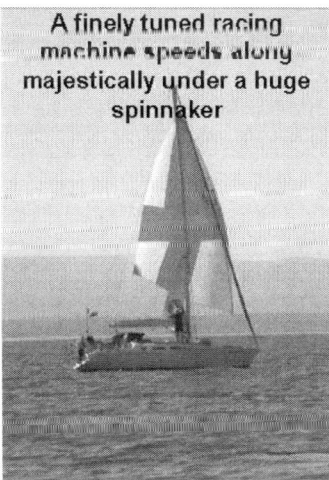
A finely tuned racing machine speeds along majestically under a huge spinnaker

The Black Prince racing to her new home

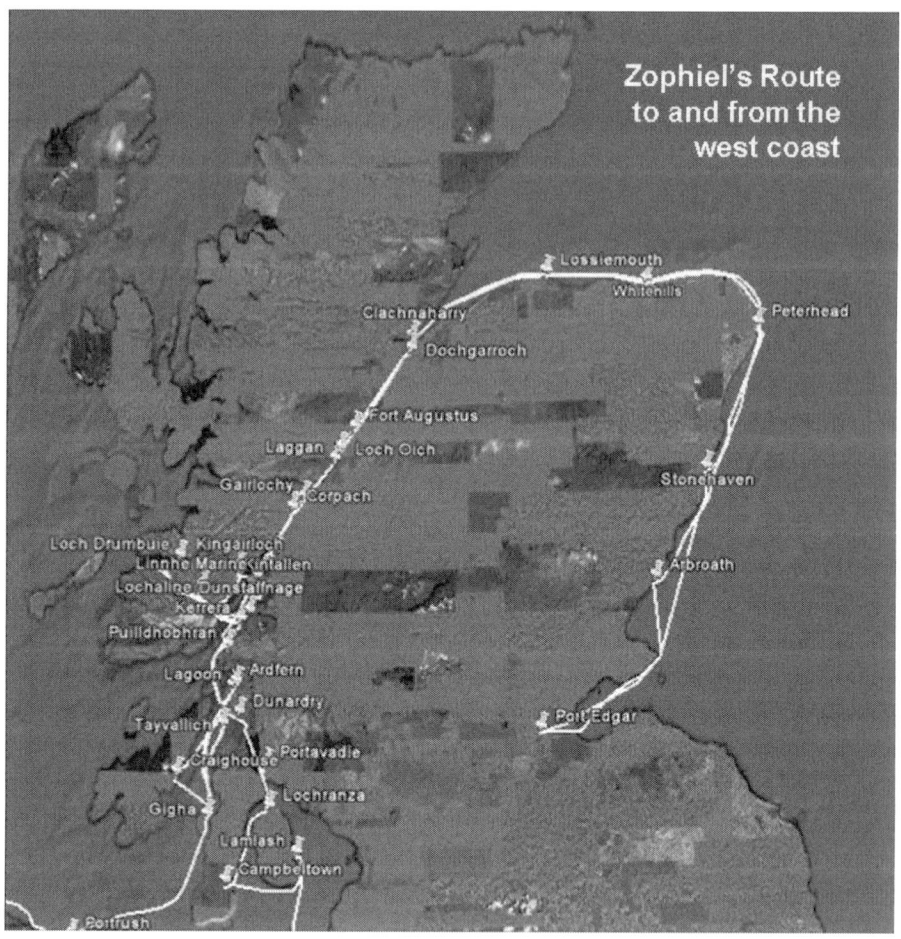

Deliverance

Haar bloody haar. The sea fog on the east coast in the spring is no joke. April 2011 had seen the whole country broiling in an unprecedented heat wave. The whole of the UK, that is, except the sea off the east coast and the pontoons at my home marina, Port Edgar, just under the Forth road and rail bridges.

On a couple of occasions I'd driven down to the marina in the baking sun, parked the car in sunshine just beside the mud flats, put on a jumper as the temperature dropped 10 degrees on the way along the main pier and been plunged into freezing winter weather – thermals, woolly hat, gloves and all – as I approached the end of the pontoon.

It finally looked as if the haar - which is what folk in Scotland call this persistent east coast sea fog - might just clear on Saturday April 23rd, as the wind was predicted to go westerly. The timing of this weather window was a little unfortunate as I am a mean bastard and had paid the marina up to the end of the month. Was it worth risking the possibility of gales or more haar and getting my extra week? A friend at the marina, Ian Cameron, decided this for me. He and Peter Lindemann were planning to take Peter's Sigma 36 *'Solpieter'* round to the west coast to take part in some madness called the 'Scottish Three Pekes Race'. Apparently Ian would be running up several mountains with a trio of lap dogs then sailing round the Mull of Kintyre against the tide in a gale. Rather them than me, but I thought I'd chum them along just for the delivery trip bit for the company.

Where to, I hadn't really decided. Three years ago I'd announced that I was going to Norway. A friend asked me how far north I'd be going. "Oh I don't know, probably up to the Lofoten Islands" I replied casually. He seemed surprised and so was I when I saw just how sodding far up north they were. So this year I was making no commitments. When asked where I was going I just said "Anstruther, but I've got charts for as far as the Canaries". Which was true. As well as a new bottom-of-the-range chartplotter I had bought a whole pile of second hand, cancelled paper charts. Nice large scale ones for Scotland – down to 1:15000 for the inner Forth, with the scale getting smaller and smaller with distance – round about 1:1,250,000 off the coast of Africa. I would probably have needed just as large scale charts for Africa, but this kind of geographical foreshortening with distance, where all the stuff nearby seems a lot bigger than the stuff a long way away, is I think quite common. It's how the BBC get away with drawing Scotland as a pimple on the top of England.

The last time Ian ~~Macaroon~~ Cameron was on my boat some idiot crashed into us and did £10,000 worth of damage, which isn't much less than Zophiel is worth. The last time I was on Ian's boat the keel fell off. So I was taking no chances. If I was to go sailing with Ian it would be on separate boats.

On the morning of April 23rd the forecast was for no more fog and gentle winds building from the south west. So early in the morning Zophiel, with my other half Anna and me on board, and Solpieter, with Ian Cameron and Pieter Lindemann, left Port Edgar motoring in, of course, a gentle easterly and thick fog. Staying out of the shipping lanes we picked our way down river. Zoph's £100 AIS receiver linked to the chartplotter proved reassuring. We tracked a ship bound for the oil refinery up the Forth at Grangemouth coming in from the fairway buoy and passing us close by in the channel. The crew of Solpieter, on the other hand, without AIS, got a good fright as they suddenly heard a foghorn close by and saw a huge shape lumbering towards them out of the pea-souper.

The start wasn't auspicious, but as we left the Forth and rounded Fife Ness the fog cleared, a breeze kicked in from the west and we sailed on a nice gentle reach to Arbroath. The downsides were that it remained cloudy and Solpieter beat us by hours, but that was the start of a near perfect delivery trip to the west coast and we didn't see much in the way of adverse conditions at all for the next twelve days.

After a showery night the next day dawned bright and sunny and we set off for the 65 mile trip to Peterhead in a flat calm. Soon we had a gentle south westerly and motorsailed for a while. As the wind increased we sailed for three hours under full sail with a poled out jib. As it died again it highlighted the frustration of sailing a slow, heavy long keeler, as Solpieter continued to make reasonable progress under sail for another couple of hours.

Sod's law dictated that as the tide went foul, the wind came back on the nose from the north east at twelve to eighteen knots, but it only got a bit cloudy and we remained chipper as we battered to Peterhead, arriving an hour or so after Solpieter. Whilst Peterhead Marina, in a corner of the large, perfectly sheltered fishing harbour, is in many ways the best place for yachts on the east coast of Britain, it is almost literally in the shadow of a maximum security prison. Notable for the number of serial killers who hail from the town, Peterhead is not Scotland's loveliest or most salubrious town.

The next morning Anna headed off back home to earn some money to keep me in the style to which I have become accustomed and the rest of us looked at the forecast. Being wimps we contemplated the batter round Rattray Head with northerly wind against tide with trepidation. Fresh in my mind was the story of another Port Edgar boat, the Contessa 32 'Marisca', whose skipper had recently to call on a Fisheries Protection Vessel for help when his liferaft was swept off the deck as he was going round Rattray Head, mostly under water. I reminded myself that Cap'n Marisca is known to be a considerable nutter when it comes to weather conditions and had probably gone when the forecast was force 9 from the north west.

Locals along the Moray Firth enjoy a rare spot of sunbathing on the beach.

Zoph at Clachnaharry Sea Lock

We had more or less decided to wait a day, despite the prospect of a soul sapping stay in this home of imprisoned psychopaths and birthplace of serial killers when Ian, observing the falling wind conditions, girded his loins and spurred us on to action.

Nervously we battered against the waves but as we rounded Rattray Head the wind died, the sun came out and we had an uneventful and pleasant delivery trip to Whitehills under motor with no wind. Well, uneventful except for my attempts to avoid colliding with Solpieter, which appeared to have her autopilot set to 'Zoph Seeking' mode. With the whole North Sea to aim at she was permanently coming up from behind, so to speak, on a collision course.

It was an easier entry into Whitehills than Ian and I had the previous autumn, when we surfed into the scary entrance in a force six northerly whilst delivering a friend's wee back from the west coast. On that occasion we had turned sharp left into the wee harbour just when it felt like we were about to founder on, ironically, the lifeboat slip. That time we were followed in by another boat from the Forth, a Beneteau 31 called *'Mrs Chippy'*. She had distinguished herself a couple of years earlier by completing the Stavanger to Banff race across the North Sea with a crew of three blokes who had three legs and three arms between them. A bit of their story is in my earlier tale 'Skagerrak and Back'.

On this latter occasion, for Zoph and Solpieter, Whitehills was a pussy cat and makes a very pleasant and secure stopover. The whole bungalow packed full of stuff for the few visiting yachts is probably the best facility for visiting yachties on the east coast.

The next day dawned bright and sunny and we got a good gentle beat for an hour or so in seven knots of wind. Then it died and we motored most of the rest of the way to Lossiemouth. This time I motored out of Whitehills without, as was the case last time, an onshore force six and a racy yacht zooming past me a couple of feet away in the fifteen metre wide channel with her go faster stripes, doing handbrake turns as though heading across the start line on a Sunday race around the cans.

Later, in full sun and on a flat sea a brand new, hyper-racy Beneteau 40 called *'The Black Prince'* passed us on her delivery trip round from the Clyde to

Port Edgar and I spoke to one of her delivery crew on the VHF for a minute. This was the Port Edgar Yacht Club Commodore's latest acquisition, in his efforts to razz yet faster round the buoys on a Sunday. There's something about putting 'The' in front of the name 'Black Prince' that makes her sound more like a Hollywood film than a yacht.

In the end the breeze got back up to ten knots and we were able to sail the last couple of miles to Lossie. On these gentle cruising trips involving, as they tend to, a lot of motoring, it's always nice to con yourself into thinking you've sailed the passage by finishing with the sails up and the engine off.

The impression of summer continued in the town, as sprogs with buckets and spades paddled off the nearby beach and ran barefoot down the streets excitedly shouting "Mummy, Mummy, why have my toes turned black" and "Mummy, Mummy I can't feel my legs". You have to be hardy when the best summer weather occurs at about five degrees centigrade.

The next day was another bright, calm, sunny day as we motored out of Lossie towards Inverness Firth. The passage was enlivened by hundreds of gannets and their chums of other species enjoying diving from height into the mirror calm sea. Around midday a wee breeze started from the north east and we reached under full sail in seven to fifteen knots of true wind.

Despite the appalling set of their tiny cruising chute, the 36ft racing yacht Solpieter almost managed to overhaul the 27ft slow cruiser Zophiel, though to their credit they did seem to be sailing as slow as possible. A few miles before Chanonry point and the entrance to Inverness Firth Solpieter's sails disappeared as she motored hard the eight miles or so to the sea lock. Enjoying the sun Zoph carried on under full sail and got there at four to five knots just nicely before the last locking time. Later Pieter crowed to the yacht club's email group about how his racing yacht had 'beaten' Zoph. He omitted to mention, however, that his magnificent victory had involved <u>motoring</u> all the way, whereas Zoph had <u>sailed</u> all the way. Mind you, they were under a considerable handicap - an inability to steer straight. This handicap caused them to run aground on the point of land just before the Clachnaharry Sea Lock. Easily done since it's only marked really clearly on all the charts and their chartplotter and echo sounder were working perfectly well.

The Inverness end of the Caledonian Canal is the Clachnaharry Sea Lock. It's a pretty spot on a nice calm evening and that's where Zoph was left on the first night by the lock keeper, a friendly chap who unaccountably calls everyone 'Mannie'. "Hello Mannie how are you doing Mannie ach that's fine Mannie well well Mannie". Solpieter, with a magnificent burst of motorised speed, had made it through the next lock and the railway bridge to Seaport Marina.

Clachnaharry earns its place in Inverness folklore from the fact that it is the last stop on the train before Inverness. Hence the phrase 'getting off at Clachnaharry' being Sneckian for coitus interruptus. The Clachnaharry Inn is destined to enter the folklore for its extraordinary anti-customer policies. The proprietor explained to Ian and Pieter, in snooty tones that echoed around the deserted tables in his empty pub, that they were full and we couldn't possibly eat there. He later served me a pint of a different (and more expensive) beer to the one I'd asked for. When I pointed out his mistake and with saintly good grace agreed to take the wrong order to save him wasting it, he remained unapologetically standing with his hand outstretched waiting for the additional 10p that the wrong beer cost. Thereby earning himself 10p, a lifetime's seething, rancorous resentment and, hopefully, shed loads of bad publicity. Getting off the train in Clachnaharry? To be honest I'd prefer coitus interruptus.

Ian and Peter headed back south, leaving Solpieter at Seaport Marina. This is one of the more annoying places to leave a boat in Scotland. When you enquire about the price the people in the office proudly crow about how theirs is the cheapest marina in Scotland, at eight quid a night per boat. In fact it's the most expensive, since you've already paid seventeen quid per metre for a 7 day licence for the canal. So leaving Zoph for a week would cost £195. It's extremely annoying to have to hand over that amount of cash to someone who keeps telling you that you ought to be pathetically grateful that it's so cheap. Adding insult to injury they call their one week pass an 'eight day licence', on the grounds that you leave on the eighth day. If you book into a hotel for one night you check out on the second day of your stay, but they don't charge you for two days.

Zoph and I spent a day or so waiting in Inverness for Anna to come back up for the weekend. She'd earned enough money to warrant a trip down the Caley Canal. This wait was enlivened by wandering the canal side squinting at boats and chandleries.

Gardening takes the place of racing for some yachties on the Caley Canal

The trimaran *'Hei Matau'* (Walter for short), was in the canal. She is another boat whose sometime home was Port Edgar. I'd last seen this frightening set of three loosely strapped together surfboards in St Lucia, after the Atlantic Rally for Cruisers in 2008. The time before that was in the Canaries and the time before that was at Port Ed, when I'd crewed on her in a gentle breeze and a flat sea. On that occasion within the space of 5 minutes we'd lost the jib, the main and the engine, done untold amounts of damage and effectively invalidated a race by sailing off with one of the race marks. Sailing her across the Atlantic would be like crossing an ocean on a Musto Skiff or ploughing a field using Shergar instead of a carthorse. She wouldn't be my choice of vessel for the job.

Another minor highlight was the man in Caley Marina, talking to a potential customer about boats for sale. He pointed out that they had easily and rapidly sold some reduced price Orkney motor boats recently. "They flew out of here" he explained. "They literally flew out of here".... "They absolutely literally flew out of here". I wish I'd been there to see that.

One of the major hazards of navigating the Caley Canal is the hordes of motor cruisers rented out each week to people the large majority of who's boat handling experience has involved manoeuvring their rubber duck around the bath. Aware of the potential damage to their fleet, hirers such as Caley Cruisers fit thick strips of black rubber all round the widest points of their scruffy, scratched, dented craft. This affords them some protection, ensures the maximum impact on the hulls of private yachts and signals clearly to their clients that they are in fact bumper-boats and the object of the game is to bump into as many things as possible. Heading up the Fort Augustus lock staircase in company with a few of these scarred nightmares can be fraught. So noticing the door of Caley Cruisers' office ajar approaching five o'clock I stuck my head in and asked when they tended to set off their hire boats. "About two thirty on Friday and Saturday. Are you on a private boat?" The girlie immediately replied. Clearly I wasn't the first concerned yachtie to ask the question.

The very first lesson given the new arrivals at Caley cruisers says it all. As they approach their new charges they see how they have been tied up by the professionals. In a row along the quay, each boat has been rammed arse-first against the concrete wall, with no fenders. holding each stern hard against the rough concrete are two piano-wire-tight lines, each about a foot long. And nothing else. On board they hop, untie the two ropes and blast off into the sunset looking for 27ft private yachts to ram.

On The Caley Canal

On the pontoon at Loch Oich

The wind only blows up or down Loch Ness, either south west or north east, so with a forecast of force three or four from the south east I confidently expected bugger-all and we motored out onto the loch. As the north east wind rose to twenty eight knots we zoomed the twenty five miles up the loch at over six knots under jib alone, gybing every now and then. For once Sod's law didn't apply and despite the forecast we had the wind behind us throughout the day. The sun condescended to stay out all day as well and we tied up to the pontoon at the bottom of the locks at Fort Augustus for the night, tucked out of the way of rogue bumper-boats.

We also managed to avoid the Caley Cruisers ascending the staircase of locks at Fort Augustus the next morning, but went in the company of a knackered old private gin palace whose driver only reluctantly turned off the massive old engines which belched black smoke into the enclosed locks. This motor boat gloried in the name 'Linda Luv', which I think paints a pretty fair picture of the boat and her crew.

The rest of the gloriously sunny day was spent slowly pootling through some locks into the shallow, island strewn Loch Oich, at the top level of the canal, where we spent the afternoon and night tied to a wee jetty. The peace was only marred by five teenagers on a bumper-boat who joined us and started getting pissed. They were, however, startlingly conservative in their habits and had shut up completely by about ten p.m. Absolutely no stamina your modern teenager. What's wrong with the youth of today?

Yet another fine, dry, sunny day saw us motoring and motorsailing down Loch Lochy and along the canal beside about a thousand cyclists on a sponsored charity ride from Fort Bill to Sneck. As we approached Corpach we experienced the perennial problem of the Fort William climate that has plagued visitors and locals alike for centuries. Dust storms. Yes, the dry weather had cyclists wearing protective masks as the gentle breeze threw up little whirlwinds of dust. In

Corpach the locals were complaining about how the drought was knackering the gardens. The local camels were dying of thirst. Ben Nevis stood clear and - I have to say - majestic on the horizon. Yes, that's right, we could actually see the whole of Ben Nevis. Against a blue sky. There are adults who have lived in Fort Bill their whole lives who have never seen Ben Nevis. That's how good the weather was on May 1st.

We practically zoomed down the eight locks of 'Neptune's Staircase' in company with a racy 36ft yacht crewed by a posh family in a hurry and settled for the night in the jewel of the west coast, Corpach, just next to the highland's only sink estate. The night was only marred by the bloody *'Lord of the Flies Isles'*, a massive converted ferry which only just fits into the locks and is the most stupid and most expensive way of experiencing the Caledonian Canal. As she arrived at the sea lock at sunset on a perfect, calm, warm evening, not one of her £2000-for-a-weekend-cruise passengers bothered coming out on deck to look at the perfect view. Needless to say the antisocial bastards kept their engines running all night, disturbing all and sundry so that a couple of geriatric American tourists could have the central heating turned up to thirty degrees centigrade and watch the telly.

The famously arid dustbowl of Fort Bill. In the far distance, on Ben Nevis, camels can be seen dying of thirst

Wild West

The next morning I packed Anna back off to Edinburgh to work, as I thought she'd had enough of a break, whilst Zoph and I headed out to sea. Just out of the sea lock my trusty old Garmin 128 GPS failed. It started beeping and failing to find any satellites. For a while I hoped that this was because the Americans had switched off the system due to impending nuclear war or some other catastrophe. At least that would mean there was nothing wrong with my machine. But no such luck and the bloody thing played up most of the way round Ireland. The folk at the marine electronics specialists at Port Edgar later helpfully explained that it was probably a bit old or something and they had no idea what was wrong with it. It wasn't exactly crucial as I had a shiny new chart plotter as well, but I'd got used to my old GPS.

I sailed through the Corran Narrows and south to Loch Creran in a fluky, gusty wind that rose during the day but still varied between force five and force zero. I sailed right into Loch Creran and on the way out met some other chums from Port Edgar. Dave Punton and Nial McHugh, the 'Odd Couple', on their Sigma 33 'Kittiwake', were motoring back in to their mooring. I had an ulterior motive for catching them as I thought my kedge anchor warp was on Kittiwake after I'd helped Dave deliver her from the Bristol Channel the previous year. The bloody thing seems to have vanished into thin air however and I came away empty handed.

I picked up a visitors' mooring at Port Appin for the night. These had previously been free if you had a pint in the hotel, but now they want a tenner for them. We are just emerging from quite a good period for picking up moorings on the west coast of Scotland. For years many of the old HIDB moorings had been unmaintained and getting more and more dodgy. More recently various pubs, hotels and community groups had been maintaining these moorings and laying more and more, offering them free to bring money into local businesses. Now they have worked out that they can also get money for them and they are getting greedier and greedier. £10 seems to have become the basic minimum, which is not bad for a mob-handed 40 footer but close to commercial rates for a wee 27 footer. Often for an exposed mooring that you need to bugger off from when the wind changes direction.

Some things are getting more free however. When I went for a walk down the peninsula a notice on gate in the middle of the track, painted roughly on a piece of plywood, said "Camping with Permission". This seemed an odd thing to write on a notice. Then I spotted the rear of the plywood. Whitewashed out yet still clearly visible was the professionally painted legend "NO CAMPING". Clearly the miserly toff who 'owned' the estate had been forced to take down the 'no camping' sign in the wake of access legislation. Travelling elsewhere in the 'Celtic Fringe' did make me appreciate how lucky we are in Scotland to be able to access the land.

The Pier House Hotel has ideas above its station. Entering the pub for a pint a wifey with airs, graces and a professional smile asked if "Sir requires a table for one". The bar no longer feels like a pub bar so much as a waiting area for a restaurant table. I sat on a bar stool feeling slightly unwelcome and failing to engage the barman in conversation.

The rural west of Scotland is littered with that most deadly of curses of local pubs, worse even than large screen tellies, the moron on a bar stool. In pub after pub a bloke, evidently a more or less permanent fixture, drones on and on about such mindless trivia as to drive the rest of the clientele away. I often wonder if this is mentioned in the particulars for prospective purchasers of pubs. "Well appointed going concern the potential of which is limited by the permanent fixture on a bar stool". I wonder if there have been any cases of such fixtures snuffing it in suspicious circumstances when landlords have been driven over the edge as their clientele is reduced to one bloke on a bar stool. Since Sir didn't require a table for one I rowed back to the boat after one desultory pint.

Another gorgeous day saw us under full sail all day past Kerrera, out to the Garvellachs and back to the lovely, sheltered and for once almost empty but still unspellable anchorage at Puilladobhrain. A fantastic day's gentle sailing in full sun, rounded off by a fine sunset in company with only two other boats. Another month or so and there would be thirty or more boats crammed together in the anchorage. I invited a chap from the nearby Ohlsen 38 on board for a beer. This was handy as he seemed to be that rarest of things, a charcoal stove nerd, who was able to tell me all about my smoky, malfunctioning stove. Apparently, it turns out to be an *'Atkey Pansy'*, though I don't know why I'm bothering to tell you that.

One more fantastic weather day as I motorsailed then sailed south down the Sound of Luing with up to four knots of tide and up to fifteen knots of breeze, but a flat sea. Right up the Dorus Mhor then a nice fast reach up to my favourite marina, Ardfern. There are several reasons why Ardfern is my favourite marina, not least amongst which are that it is open, with no high walls round it and doesn't really feel like a marina at all. It's also cheap for visitors in small yachts. This comes as a bit of a surprise once you've clocked all the posh boats on 'millionaire's row'. Ardfern charge for moorings by the metre, which is handy if you have a 27 footer. At Ardfern the cost of a commercial mooring with all facilities where you can happily leave your boat is less than the 'nominal charge' made for some of the most expensive club moorings in piss-poor bays with neither facilities nor shelter.

The weather was finally due to break so I decided to leave Zoph at Ardfern for a few days. I left brimming with confidence about the long hot summer ahead and all the time I would have to get round Ireland - and possibly further. It was only May the fourth and I was already at a jumping-off point for Ireland. I hadn't expected to have left Port Ed until the start of May so I was well ahead of schedule. A couple of days at home and I'd be back to enjoy more glorious weather and a fantastic early summer. The month of May stretched ahead of me invitingly.

By June the boat was still in Ardfern. I'd not progressed a single solitary inch. May was a total meteorological disaster. The only thing to be said in its favour is that at least I didn't have to sit on the boat enduring its endless gales and downpours. At least I could get on with something else instead of sailing.

I did come back during May and have another go. On May the thirteenth, which was of course a Friday, there was a tiny chink in the forecast. A miniscule bright window of weather in which it might be possible to sail appeared in the long dark tunnel of storm clouds which otherwise stretched until the end of time.

Before I left Ardfern I headed for the fuel berth. First I had to wait for two hippies - an Anglo-Japanese couple - in a scruffy old 32ft ketch - to vacate the berth. They live aboard, almost always at anchor, on the west coast all year, making ends meet by collecting shellfish in the intertidal zone. This they sell directly to dealers at the quayside. I'm not sure I'd fancy the January gales on an anchor. Never being able to leave your house for more than an hour in case it blew away in a blizzard would not breed a sense of relaxed security. But each to their own.

As they vacated the berth some oldsters in an immaculate - and extraordinarily expensive looking - Grand Banks motorsailer muscled in and got on the fuel berth ahead of me. On my last visit I'd seen one of the lads employed by Ardfern scrubbing away with a toothbrush at a tiny bit of algae that had grown in the join between the hull and the glossy teak nameplate. Clearly the owners weren't short of a bob or two. As the marina manny filled up their twin 1000 litre tanks he told me who owned it. It was the son of a famous Blair, who lived off the Blair estate, which presumably still brings in a fair amount of dosh. The Blair concerned wasn't wanted for war crimes and it wasn't Lionel. Any other ideas? You'll have to read to the end for the answer. Or you could, I suppose, just turn to the back. Damn! I never thought of that.

Given that it's cheap, Ardfern doesn't half attract a lot of posh stuff. Top of the toffs list is Anne Phillips-Laurence, nee Windsor, who kept a Rustler 36 there. I understand she's now traded it in for something bigger, which is undeniable a good use of taxpayers' money. There's so many Rustler 36s at Ardfern that it's hard to tell which one is hers. Presumably a lot of sub-toffs buy them in an effort to keep up with the Windsors.

Posher still was one of the boats at Craobh Haven, a walk away north over the hill. Tied to the end of one trot of pontoons was the ketch *'Northern Spirit'*. Its bow protruded four metres past one finger pontoon, it stretched the full length of the pontoon, across the main pontoon, the full length of the opposite finger and its stern stuck out another four metres. It was 122 feet long and its mizzen mast, much smaller than the main mast, made the mast of a nearby Moody 54 sloop look pathetically tiny. It was blinking huge. Walking on the pontoon I was not tall enough to see on deck. Its flag was the size of Zoph's mainsail.

In the on-site pub I asked about it. Nobody there seemed to have noticed it and when I pointed it out they found it unremarkable. The barmaid said it belonged to a young Kiwi couple who were cruising about on it. Given that it flew a red ensign, must have cost many millions and yet had disgorged a couple of rusting bikes and a box of flip-flops onto the pontoon, I guessed that the Kiwi couple were some of the crew and had been winding the barmaid up. "No, no" she said, "they own it and are just cruising about visiting friends". She didn't seem to find this in any way remarkable. In reality Northern Spirit is owned by a company and you can charter her from as little as €52,000 a week. But the Kiwis must have had fun pretending to own her and living it up in between corporate charters. At 122ft, by the way, she sleeps six, which seems to me like poor use of space.

On May the fourteenth I headed off down the Sound of Jura making for Gigha under full sail. The wind was a light north easterly, but it rose during the day until, by the time I was closing on the McCormack Isles off the entrance to Loch Sween it was pretty much a proper force six. With a couple of reefs in this was fine, except that I was - perhaps foolishly - towing the dinghy. Once this had flipped over a total of thirty four times I decided enough was enough and headed up Loch Sween for Tayvallich. To add to the excitement, as I was close hauled up the loch I noticed that one of the gas rings on the cooker had been knocked onto full on and the boat was full of deadly butane. Since the charcoal stove was burning I assumed that the concentration of gas wasn't great enough to have caused a fatal explosion, so we sailed the rest of the way with all hatches open and me pumping madly on the bilge pump.

This was also the day of the Scottish Three Pekes race. I phoned Ian Macaroon whilst the pekes were running up a mountain on Jura. The crew of Solpieter were contemplating a run round the fabled Mull of Kintyre in a following force six and hoping to get round before the tide changed. In the event the timing was good and they made it round in good time.

An old 12m yacht called *'Sceptre'* wasn't so fortunate. Having run aground on Jura and suspecting that they had done some damage, they left their pre-pubescent runners from a posh public school ashore on Jura and retired from the race. Unaccountably, for some reason, they then decided to sail off round the Mull on *'Septic'* in a rising force six against the tide. Unsurprisingly the place where they lost all steerage was just off the Mull and they needed both the Campbeltown lifeboat and a big naval shooty-ship to tow them into port. They were reported to have been 'unlucky' to lose steerage as they did. I wouldn't claim any great expertise in the matter but weren't they just daft to have set off in such conditions on a damaged boat, as opposed to being unlucky?

Tayvallich looks like the most perfect natural harbour possible. It's the twee-est of villages surrounding a perfect round pool a few hundred yards across and about four metres deep. Having dragged the anchor, with 35m of chain, right through the moorings twice in an easterly in the past, I knew it wasn't actually that perfect. There's three visitor moorings and visitor pontoons now and since it was only the beginning of May a mooring was available. Tayvallich is one of the clubs that claims to charge a 'nominal sum' for their moorings. At ten squid a night the three moorings are fully occupied all summer and at fifteen quid a night the pontoons do a brisk trade, netting them an estimated £5000 a year. I don't object to people running commercial, profit making operations, but I do wish they wouldn't pretend that they are a bleedin' charity and go on about 'nominal' charges. I mentioned this to the Tayvallich moorings police, who explained that the income from visitors had to pay the full costs of all the pontoon facilities. I asked if the pontoon was primarily for the use of local members, not the visitors who were paying for it. 'Yes' he said. I pointed out that on that basis they were actually making a profit. He had difficulty with this concept. I pointed out that if I charged thousands of pounds for services rendered, then claimed that I wasn't making a profit on it and that it was a charitable act on the grounds that I had to pay for my house, my car, my food, my boat and holidays in the Bahamas out of it, this wouldn't cut much ice. The blank look grew marginally blanker.

That nice calm, quiet night was marred by the screaming engines which blared out over the bay all night, from dusk to dawn, bouncing off the hills and houses and echoing out over the water. In the morning I was able to establish that this racket had been caused by a fisherman on a small boat in the harbour. It was, apparently, important for him to run two generators all the time to watch the football and then keep the cabin lights on all night. Presumably he was afraid of the dark.

Disturbed on another mooring was a Westerly Tempest from Holyhead. I asked the couple on board if they knew my Uncle John, who in his eighties continued to sail an old Hallberg Rassy out of the club there. "Yes, I know John", said the bloke. "I often enjoy sitting in the club bar at Holyhead spending hours talking to him". "Well, corrected his wife", *"listening* to him". John did tend to have fixed and complicated opinions about things. I wonder how we can possibly be related.

The weather window had collapsed suddenly and without warning like a Microsoft one and I ended up staying three nights in Tayvallich as forecasts in excess of force six from the south west continued not to amount to anything, but the weather remained universally wet and horrible. In the end I gave it up as a bad job and motorsailed back to Ardfern in a lull in the wind but in persistent drizzle. I left the boat on the same mooring as before and buggered off back to Edinburgh to observe the closely packed isobars sweeping in from the west in wave after wave which completely knackered the whole of May. The week beginning May the twenty third saw apocalyptic winds - the biggest anyone could remember - bringing untold damage at sea and on shore, scorching all the leaves, turning all the trees brown and bringing autumn to the west coast of Scotland and Ireland six months early. The signs were not good. From being well ahead of the game we were now approaching June and with south-westerly gales Ireland might as well be the other side of the Atlantic.

It was June the second before another window opened and even that looked like it might get jammed and painted shut. Early on the morning of June the second I headed out of Ardfern and south for Gigha in no wind but a dreich drizzle that seemed to sum up that early summer, my mood and the chances of actually ever getting to Ireland. Why was I bothering to plough on south in the freezing damp when I'd just end up turning tail and heading back? The ominous swirly tides around the Dorus Mhor just added to the sense of underworld gloom.

But the breeze picked up from the north east and slowly, very slowly, the day cleared. The wind stayed on the quarter and as I turned east of south round the McCormack Isles - the only islands in Scotland owned by a political party (the Scot Nats), it backed conveniently to keep me on a perfect reach. As I picked up one of the fifteen or so visitors' buoys at Gigha the sky cleared completely, the sun shone and it turned into an utterly perfect summer's day.

Gigha has the same sort of peculiarly attractive quality as Iona, which the dim-witted ascribe to 'an aura of spirituality'. "The quality of the light", they say, "is indescribably different due to the uniquely deep religiosity of the place". In reality, of course, it's more simple. Both Iona and Gigha have shallow, sandy-bottomed sea, giving them a turquoise colour and making the light bright and full of colour. For the frustrated middle class nutty tourist in search of god, he seems to reside, like lugworms, in a shallow sandy sea. There's relatively few places with this sort of sandy bottom where you can anchor securely. A sandy shore usually means a windswept lee shore. Us yachties are condemned forever to anchor on gloopy mud and leave the deep spirituality of a shallow sandy bottom to more enlightened folk. Gigha is an exception, as long as the wind stays in the west. As soon as it blows from the east you know all about lee shores, as I've discovered on a couple of previous occasions.

This time however, oddly given the conditions of the past month or so, the gentle breeze remained benignly in the west. My luck was holding well that night. Down the pub a local told me that was the last night before they started charging ten quid a night for their dodgy moorings, which are untenable as soon as the wind shifts.

Cranium

It cannot have escaped your notice that Ireland looks like a huge baby. The map of Ireland that is. Therefore those of you for whom, like me, its geography is something of a mystery, need not despair. Given that Ireland is just the next door bit of land my knowledge of its layout is shamefully poor. I know lots of names of towns and counties but couldn't for the life of me place them on a map. Like most people I sort of assumed that 'Northern Ireland' took up much of the north of Ireland. In reality it's just the top north east corner.

To assist us in our geographical ignorance, it obviously helps to think of Ireland as a huge struggling baby, with its head facing Britain but its arms and legs straining out into the Atlantic trying to get away. I'm not sure how well the metaphor stands up politically (actually not too badly perhaps, given their history and apparent love affair with America), but the physical resemblance is clear. Lough Neagh is the baby's large eye, Strangford Lough its nostrils, Carlingford Lough its mouth. Donegal is the cranium, counties Mayo and Galway the arms, Kerry and Cork the legs and Rosslare, appropriately enough, the arsehole. For your convenience the rest of my cruise round Ireland is therefore described in these helpful anatomical terms.

The weather continued perfect and sunny the next day in what the media began referring to without apparent irony as a 'heat wave'. I'm not entirely sure that two days without rain qualifies as a heat wave. Perhaps that's symptomatic of how crap our recent summers have been and how low our expectations have become.

With bugger all wind and in full sun we motored south, getting some benefit from the flood tide towards Rathlin Island and crossing the shipping lanes just ahead of a big scary tanker coming in from the west. Two yachts passed me heading north as the marinas of Northern Ireland emptied into the west of Scotland for the summer, as is their wont. The idea was to get to Rathlin at about slack water and turn west, getting the benefit of the ebb to Portrush, the last coastal port before Loch Foyle and the

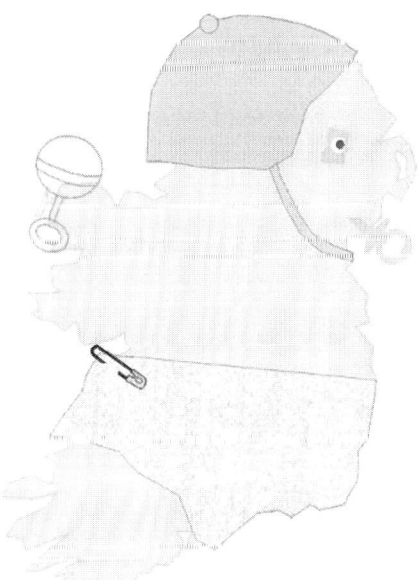

There's no political agenda here.
Ireland just does look like a big baby.

Irish Republic. It only just didn't quite work properly and I had an hour or so of tide against me before it turned and I motored on a glassy sea the 46 miles to Portrush. There I tied up on the single long pontoon just behind a dirty great English tall ship whose crew were making ends meet by taking locals for trips round the bay.

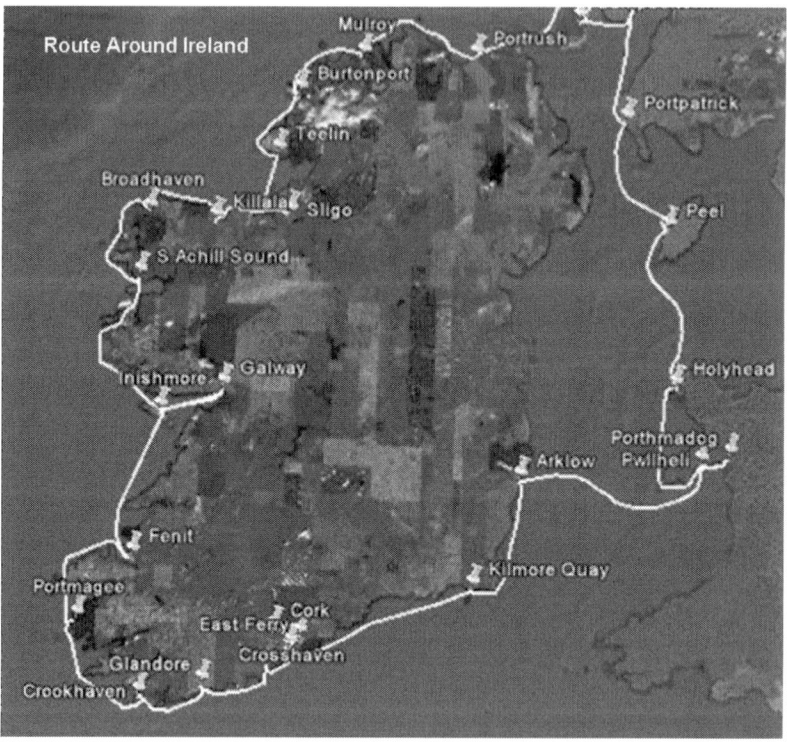

In Portrush, just above Ireland's hairline, I was soon joined by two local yachts from Coleraine en route to Rathlin for a party. Their skippers dragged me kicking and screaming to the pub where we spoke to quite a number of the local yachtie populace. I asked them all about the coast further west and they all looked at me blankly. None of them had the slightest idea what it was like cruising westward beyond the river Bann. That was the Republic and they all cruised north and east to Scotland. They were extremely friendly and one bloke even tried to press upon me his brand new pilot book of Northern and Eastern Coasts of Ireland (my copy is about a decade old), going home to fetch it and insisting that I take it with me. None of them, however, knew anything about the coast further west. Instead they regaled me with stories about Islay and Gigha, Jura and Mull, Skye and onwards to the north. To them the west of Scotland was their back yard and their local cruising ground, a short hop away across the dodgy North Channel. For them the Celtic Fringe was real enough - they identified closely with the islands to the north. But whether for deeply held political reasons or just because Scottish waters are a more sheltered cruising ground than Irish waters, they were blind to anything further west.

I had observed this before - this close affinity which the boating community of Northern Ireland feel for Scotland. An awful lot of them don't have yachts but fast ribs. These are called things like *'Sanda'* and *'Eriskay'* and they take their owners on quick trips over to the pub in what we would consider to be practically another country. Many of their owners live on the north coast of Ireland and from the sofas in their five bedroomed commuter houses, an hour from Belfast, ranged along the cliff tops facing north, they can clearly see Islay and the Mull of Kintyre. To most of us in Scotland, Northern Ireland feels a long way - possibly even an aeroplane flight - away. To many of the Northern Irish, Scotland forms the permanent backdrop to their lives. We are their neighbours but, paradoxically, they aren't our neighbours. It's as though there's a huge one-way mirror somewhere in the North Channel. They look over at us and see our every move. We hardly ever notice that they are there. A trip to the Northern Irish coast gives a first inkling of the interconnectedness of the Celtic lands. For us in the Central Belt England perhaps seems like our nearest neighbour. By sea its a million miles away whilst Ireland is a mere stones throw.

Rathlin Island, first contact with Ireland

Encouraged by the friendliness of the Northern Irish, I was looking forward to hitting Eire. With its legendary friendly people and Guinness I felt I was assured of a warm welcome. The weather didn't look too friendly however and seemed set to cut up rough. After our two day 'heat wave' normal service was to be resumed. It was cloudy and sometimes dreich and whilst the wind was only going to be about a force five, it would be right on the nose all the way to Malin Head, after which we would be in the proper North Atlantic, with permanent westerly swell and, in this instance, a two knot tide against the swell to turn it nice and vertical and choppy. With this in mind I looked at other options for ports in Eire but before the dreaded Malin Head. Lead contender was Greencastle, a port on the west side of Loch Foyle. To see what this friendly little port was like for yachts I Googled "Yachts Greencastle" and this was the first result the computer threw up...

"IRISH TIMES MAY 20TH 2011 - "<u>Anger as three yachts denied port in</u>

Donegal storm"

"THREE YACHTS were denied shelter from a storm in a Co Donegal port by protesters claiming to protect the rights of fishermen, the chairman of the county council said. The yachts, from France, Sweden and Buncrana, Co Donegal, were stopped from entering Greencastle harbour on May 7th after high winds forced them to seek shelter. It is understood the boats had come in as far as the pontoon but, after suffering verbal abuse from protesters, the crews were forced to put to sea in the stormy conditions."

"Oh well that's just frigging brilliant" I thought. "Not only North Atlantic storms ahead but also severe beatings by insane sodding fishermen. So much for legendary frigging Irish friendliness".

I decided to head round the Head instead.

Malin Head is of course a famous one. It gives its name to a shipping forecast sea area and crops up time and again - usually something to do with hyper-strong winds and high seas. For me it was the first of seemingly countless 'Heads' I needed to get round. The north and west of Ireland has a deeply indented coastline, the nooks and crannies of which I hoped to explore. But the corollary of deep indentations is exposed sticky-out bits, each of which had to be got round. Many of these figure large in the Irish coastal forecasts, which give you the weather from headland to headland. Names like Fair Head, Howth Head, Erris Head, Slyne Head, Loop Head, Mizen Head and the portentously named Bloody Foreland would figure large in my life over the next few weeks, as I listened to the prophets of doom at Met Eireann on the VHF. Sailing round Ireland would seem like a major headland a day and the indented bits of the crinkles, in the oxters and elbows, were largely passed by.

But the first one was Malin Head. I headed off to windward under full sail but against a couple of knots of tide. Reaching the other way came a fleet of boats out of the River Bann, predictably heading north east towards Scotland. As the tide turned progress was better, but the seas became more vertical with wind over tide. For a while I was just about making Malin Head under sail, but soon the engine went on and a couple of reefs went in as I plugged away against the swell. Malin Head was theoretically the last of the big tides - beyond there the tidal flow round the coast is not strong - but it was also the first of the Atlantic swells.

All along the west and north coast of Ireland - and to a lesser extent the south coast - the Atlantic swell is more or less a permanent fixture. If there's ten knots of wind there's a metre and a half of swell. This means you can't really sail as the rolling of the boat makes it impossible to set the sails and the boom crashes from side to side. As the wind increases to fifteen knots you get to sail for ten minutes. Then the swell increases to two metres and you're back to square one. The same happens as the wind increases to twenty knots. Downwind on a broad reach you can just about sail if the wind is strong enough.

Two items of the rig became permanent fixtures round the coast of Ireland, a boom preventer and a safety line. The preventer was a single long line, led from the cockpit outside everything, through two blocks on the pulpit and back to the cockpit. One end was then tied to the boom and the other tightened on the winch for the lazy jib sheet. To change tack, untie the preventer from the boom and tie on the other end. This was an absolutely essential piece of kit to avoid the boom crashing back and forth and causing crash gybes as the boat pitched and rolled in the swell. I even used it when, like that first day round Malin Head, we were going to windward.

A random photo of the Irish coast just to show how dreich it was and why there aren't more photos in this bit

The only point of a lifejacket for single handed sailing is to clip a safety line to. All the annoying mantras about lifejackets ('useless unless worn') we are currently bombarded with completely gloss over the fundamental uselessness of the device to the single-handed sailor. What the hell is the point of bobbing about in freezing seas and a three metre swell somewhere off Malin Head for ten minutes before you drown? It would be far more useful if the RNLI and others hammered home the message 'Don't fall in'. If, as a single handed sailor in a deserted sea you fall in, you're as good as dead. So the only point of a lifejacket is to clip a safety line to. This I did most of the way round the north and west coasts. Wet gear and wellies were absolutely necessary every day as the constant spray soaked me, and the lifejacket was, for once, also a constant as I clipped on even just to sit in the cockpit. I wonder how many people have toppled off a boat partly lulled into a false sense of security by their reassuring but largely useless lifejacket.

In what would become a recurring pattern my GPS VMG to Malin Head decreased and decreased as the swell grew choppier in the force four or five north westerly and we had to motorsail further and further off the wind to maintain progress against the waves. Finally however we were round and able to bear away towards Mulroy Harbour, a deeply indented hole in the top of the baby's head, just west of the much larger trepanning of Loch Swilly. The unfortunately named Fanny's Bay, halfway up Mulroy Harbour, was billed in the pilot book as the best anchorage on the coast and it probably would be were it not mostly filled with moorings. Forty nine miles from Portrush we picked our way through the rocks and up the narrow channel against the strong tide to the excellently sheltered bay, part of an extensive area of shallow, sheltered inland water.

I was circling around the bay looking for a suitable anchoring spot when I heard Zoph's name on the radio. It was a fisherman on a nearby lobbo-boat advising me which of the local moorings to pick up. I thanked him and picked up the mooring. This was my first taste of what Irish fishermen are really like and how they really react to visiting yachts. I was pleased at how calm the sheltered bay was after all the stories I'd read about the swell on this coast and its ability to find its way into any anchorage. Being a lazy git I didn't go ashore. There's no way I could tow a dinghy round this coast, with its Atlantic swells, so going ashore meant blowing it up then deflating and re-stowing it. This is the downside of a cutter rig without stowage room on the foredeck.

Posh new houses in Burtonport

The next day the weather was diabolical - pissing down all day. It seemed appropriate for a passage round today's daily headland, the frighteningly named Bloody Foreland. But for once the wind cooperated, starting in the north east and backing handily to the north-north west as I turned southwards. I sailed all day in a semicircle with the wind always 130 to 140 degrees on the starboard side. In the pissing rain and very poor visibility, with fifteen to twenty knots of wind on the quarter I headed under full sail towards the equally distressingly named Tory Island. I had intended, with some reluctance, to stop there for the night. The rather dull sail, during which I hardly saw any of the land a mile or so away, was enlivened by Test Match Special on long wave.

As I approached Tory Island, Ireland's dandruff, a couple of yachts could just be seen through the mist and rain heading in the opposite direction. I was to see nearly bugger-all sign of anyone else cruising for the next eight days or so.

Tory Island would have been nice and sheltered in a north westerly, but the forecast was for the wind to go back to the south the next day, so I decided to press on round the corner. We sailed round Bloody Foreland, off the pages of the

Irish Cruising Club's 'East and North Coast of Ireland' Pilot and onto the pages of their South and West Coasts volume. This, as always, I was to sail right through backwards, moving ever nearer to the front of the book and trying to reverse their descriptions of passages in my head so that they made sense. The pilot book claims that it's becoming more and more popular to circumnavigate Ireland. I was to conclude over the next week or so that this meant that one boat did it in 2010 and two boats were doing it in 2011.

On a broad reach we sailed inside Aranmore Island, which I had only just realised was not the famous and much touristed Aran, to the small, scruffy fishing port of Burtonport. The entrance to Burtonport was reminiscent of Norway, with the houses built right down to the rocky shore of a narrow, winding channel like a perfectly sheltered seagoing street. Like in Norway I had the sensation of driving the boat up side streets like a car. As so often in Norway I was buzzed in the channel by ro-ro ferries constantly scuttling in and out of the port and speeding up the narrow waterways.

The ferries, which berthed on a rough slip in the little port, were called *'Morvern'*, *'Coll'* and *'Rhum'*. Later I established that they were indeed ex CalMac vessels, recently purchased. It is of course well known that the overwhelming egomania of the directors of Caledonian MacBrayne means that they won't use anything smaller than the QE2 to ferry two blokes and a goat to islands with a population of twelve. The apparently bottomless pit of public funding for their excesses means they never have to. I'm almost surprised they didn't just scuttle Morvern, Coll and Rhum, such is their disdain for matters of mere economics and small ferries.

Though the approach was intriguing the actual port and village of Burtonport was a bit of a disappointment. The rather old pilot book talks of a town full of pubs, restaurants and shops. Now there's one pub, one restaurant and a petrol station a mile away where you can buy a pint of milk. There's an abandoned, derelict supermarket and a couple of deserted, boarded up pubs. It's a place that really looks like it's suffering in the wake of Ireland's current economic problems. I rather expected this run-down, decaying atmosphere to be a recurring theme in Ireland, but in fact it wasn't and of my limited sample of places Burtonport seemed one of the few that looked really run down. There were plenty of people about, but since this was a Sunday evening all of them drove at speed off the constant stream of ferries from Aranmore and shot off eastwards.

An enterprising van selling wet fish and weight training

My previous experience of Irish ports had been the hugely overpriced, glossy and officious marinas around Dublin at Howth and Dunlaoghaire (pronounced Dun-lee-oggee-hairy) and these did not prepare me at all for Burtonport. A few scruffy fishing boats lined the harbour walls and on the advice of a hailed fisherman I tied Zoph to the outside of a small raft. This raft consisted of a 25ft lobster boat, outside which was a half-deflated eighteen foot rib, outside which was a sixteen foot wooden rowing boat half full of water, outside which was Zoph. I voiced my concerns at this arrangement to various fishermen, who shrugged, said she'd be fine and pointed me in the direction of the 'Harbourmaster', an old bloke at the other end of the harbour bailing out another small lobster boat. I introduced myself and asked if I could stay where I was. "If you want, that's fine" he said. Or should I move outside a couple of bigger fishing boats? "If you want, that's fine" he said. Or perhaps I should move to a short free part of the wall next to the ferries. "If you want, that's fine" he said. I asked if he wanted any money for berthing. He seemed to find this an odd question and I had my first of many absolutely free nights snug in perfectly secure, sheltered harbours.

As I spoke to the local fishermen there was absolutely no sense whatever of seething resentment against yachties. As the days passed I realised that this was probably because there aren't any yachts.

Rural Ireland hasn't been as depopulated as the west of Scotland – A village round every headland

Rafted up in Teelin

Neck and Shoulder

Monday morning and normal service was resumed. The weather was still fairly miserable - full cloud cover and showers - but the wind was now firmly in the south south west. Twenty knots right on the nose. For about a second I sailed. Then for six hours I battered into the wind and swell with two reefs in the main and the staysail set, motorsailing at about fifty degrees to the apparent wind as the only feasible way of plugging through the eight to ten foot waves. It was a damp and uncomfortable passage with the VMG to today's headland, Malin More, teetering around the three knot mark for twenty five miles. At the start I saw one bloke out in a wee open boat, then a large fishing boat being shadowed by a coastguard helicopter on exercises, then nothing at all for the rest of the day.

Finally we passed Malin More and bore away. The jib was unfurled and we sailed. But soon we had to bear away again to put the wind 130 degrees to starboard and again sailing was impossible. Again it seemed as though there were virtually no conditions of wind strength and direction on the west of Ireland that allow you to sail. You can't sail close hauled because the rolling keeps luffing the sails and you are battering into the waves. You can't sail with the wind over 120 apparent as the rolling causes the boom to batter about. You can't sail in ten to twelve knots of wind as you need more power to fill the sails in the rolling. As the wind increases you can sail temporarily, until the sea state increases with the wind and the rolling increases. I concluded that the conditions for sailing are... Wind between about 90 and 120 degrees true - that is a total of sixty of the possible 360 degrees – only in rising wind speeds between fourteen and twenty four knots, for about the first five minutes of that wind strength. In other words, nearly never.

As we bore away round Malin More and inside Rathlin O'Birne Island the heavens opened and it absolutely pissed down for two hours as the wind increased and we surged along at hull speed for a minute. Apparently Teelin, just at the bottom end of the back of Ireland's hairdo, lays claim to the tallest sea cliffs in Europe. I suppose I must have sailed right past them within about a quarter of a mile, but I never saw a bloody thing with visibility through the rain at about two hundred metres. I later discovered that quite a number of places along this coast claim to have the highest cliffs in Europe. Let's be charitable and say there's genuinely different ways of measuring their height.

With a southerly swell I was worried as I arrived somewhat knackered that the small, open harbour of Teelin would be exposed. All writers about cruising the west of Ireland refer to the incessant swell making anchorages unpleasant.

But in fact the swell dropped away remarkably quickly as I entered the bay behind a trip boat which had taken tourists out squinting at cliffs. Not being easily able to identify the supposed visitors' buoys I asked the trip boat skipper if I could tie outside his boat for the night. He was fantastically accommodating, taking my lines, offering the lend of extra fenders, helping with berthing and giving me chapter and verse on all the local attractions. Teelin was in fact a great taster of just how fantastically friendly the western Irish are to visitors. It's a bit of a cliché but it really was true that the highlight of my trip was the people and their friendliness. A great change from the miserable bastards one generally meets in Britain.

It had stopped raining and the evening was quite pleasant so I walked the mile and a half up the hill along pleasant lanes above the calm bay to the local pub and discovered the dangers of making casual observations in Ireland. I said that it was nice that they had an open fire as a lot of my clothes were wringing wet. The landlady practically insisted that I bring all my washing to the pub to dry in front of the fire. She was beside herself with what amounted to grief that I would be gone the next day so couldn't bring in all my washing.

I mentioned that phone reception wasn't very good and that I'd walk up the hill to where it was better. The Landlord practically insisted that I use their landline, even after I'd explained it was an international call and would cost half the Irish National debt. When I was walking up the hill a passing van stopped. It was the Landlord again, insisting that I go back to the pub and ask his wife for the use of the phone. It was like this all along the west coast. People being genuinely friendly and interested in what you are doing. Back in the pub an octogenarian local told me a sad tale about how he could never really get on with the sea since his son was drowned in it many years before.

A north westerly gale was forecast for two days time, so the next day I knew I needed to head for somewhere nice and secure. Being a wimp I always seem to run for cover too early and spend days waiting for the forecast bad conditions. The nearby Killibegs, Ireland's busiest fishing port, was one option, as was heading right across Donegal Bay the fifty miles or more to the open anchorage of Broadhaven. I took the wimp's route and headed south and a bit west to Sligo, on Ireland's shoulder, where there was rumoured to be an actual pontoon, miles from the sea up a winding tidal river.

The day was brighter as I motored with full sail and the boom preventer on in the rolly sea with about ten knots of wind. The swell finally subsided as I entered the sheltered bay in the approach to Sligo and the engine went off as I ran in under full sail past the sailing club moorings at Rosses Point. There's strong tidal flows here making anchoring uncomfortable, so I left behind the few scruffy racers and dayboats moored in what is billed as a major sailing centre. The village at Rosses point looked quite nice with some rather swanky houses down to the water, but the boats looked like they did little more than nip round the cans in the bay on August bank holiday.

The pilot book doesn't bother to mention that the channel up river to Sligo should be taken at high tide and of course I attempted it at lowish tide, albeit on the flood. Parts of the centre of this four mile long shipping channel between training walls were exposed mud. Navigation wasn't helped by the yellow cans right down the centre of the marked channel which, I think, were to encourage you down one side of the channel, which was the deep half. But since they were yellow and in the middle you just had to guess which half. We hit soft mud and slowed right down a couple of times, but with her 1.4 metre draught

Zoph pushed through and we arrived at the long municipal pontoon on which various wee local boats were rafted up three deep. I'd not taken into account the fact that this was a river, so made a right arse of coming alongside in the two knot current, but was helped by a South African 'local' hippy getting pissed on a wee local folkboat with his elderly and extraordinarily hairy chum. In Ireland as in Britain white South Africans seem to have made their home and got citizenship, for some reason, wherever there's a useful cricket team or no significant black population.

Also on the pontoon was the only other cruising boat I'd seen on this coast, a Sigma 41 crewed by five old blokes from Preston who were going round Ireland the opposite way to me. 'The right way', as they observed. They were friendly and I went to the pub for a pint with them, trying to ignore the loud, bizarre and misinformed views on Scottish economics and politics, which all English people now seem to have adopted and be keen to impart.

Sligo is one of those Irish county towns which we've all heard of but which I, for one, could not have remotely hoped to be able to place on the map. Pleasant and mostly unremarkable, it has been responsible for two towering literary giants, being the birthplace of WB Yeats and Spike Milligan's dad.

Plenty of evidence of euro-money in Sligo – a new art gallery extension

Ireland's gayest statue

You will doubtless be wondering about ablutions. You will perhaps assume that out of a sense of decorum I have fallen short of describing in minute detail my washing arrangements. This is not strictly true. No details are too minor or boring for me to inflict them upon you. The truth is that I'd not managed a shower for a large number of days. The lack of such facilities is a feature of this coast. In Sligo however there was a hotel which was rumoured to provide showers for a fee. When I arrived the twelve year old girl behind reception gave me, without apparent levity, the key to Room 101. She looked puzzled when I asked what fearful abomination I could expect to find there. Would it be a yawning, vertiginous chasm, the cast of Celebrity Big Brother or Jeremy bloody Clarkson? Mind you, that mightn't be such a bad thing if I was also furnished with a gun...

In the event Room 101 held none of my deepest fears, only a crap shower. In fact the shower in this three star hotel room was completely cold, there was no shower screen at all and no plug for the bath. So I had to wash sitting in the bath with my toe in the plug hole using the detachable spray thingy from the wash basin. Such are the trials of the cruising sailor. Happily the girl on reception was too dim either to understand the significance of Room 101 or to charge me for the shower.

I spend two nights and a whole pleasant, if windy day in Sligo. Like most Irish towns the Tourist Information was helpful and self-guided walks low key and interesting. Three signs caught my attention. A notice in a shop doorway that read "Back in five minutes, traphic permitting (there should be no 'f' in traphic)" was one. Another was the plaque erected to Leo Milligan and the third a plaque erected, bizarrely, by the Chilean Government in honour of Sligo notables Ambrosio O'Higgins and his son, Bernardo O'Higgins, first President of Chile.

As in many parts of Scotland the recent Polish influence seems large. Not only are there several Polish shops, but one supermarket had everything – its name, prices, opening times, adverts etc – except the word 'Welcome', written in Polish. In this apparently Gaelic speaking area with the usual overdone Gaelic road signs there's clearly a lot more people who speak Polish than Gaelic.

It looks like there's been plenty of money in Sligo. There's recently built expensive looking houses and a massive art gallery extension built at huge cost to quadruple the size of the original gallery and, in the modern way, show about four pictures. But Sligo does look like the economy is on its way down. One five bedroomed, newly renovated house in an estate agent's window was advertised as having been reduced from €325,000 to €225,000. The old mannies from Preston all thought that house prices were expensive in Sligo, which probably says a lot about the economy of Preston.

This time I did get charged for berthing, but the lad in the Harbour Office, in a uniform complete with gold braid, seemed reluctant to charge for two nights, explaining, for some reason, that the Harbourmaster was away at the TT. Eventually he charged rather less than the published rate. This reluctance to take money seemed to be a recurrent theme. In Britain a public sector employee such as a harbourmaster would have had it explained to him in no uncertain terms that his job was on a shoogly peg and relied on him bringing in income. The public sector is often more rapaciously capitalist than the private sector. This attitude doesn't seem to have arrived in the west of Ireland... yet. There, three people sit all day in a tourist information office in a town with no tourists and the harbourmaster can't really be bothered with the complication of charging visitors because it interferes with his fishing.

Surfers at the entrance to Killala

Shoulder Arms

Once the gale had blown out I set off again. From having been in a position to get directly to Broadhaven, just before Erris Head, three days before, I was now faced with a two day beat westwards, against what remained of the wind and the swell left over from the north westerly gale. This illustrates a problem with this coast, the dangers of heading east up its major inlets and the reason why I missed out on so many good sheltered cruising areas in its deep indentations. My first destination was the fishing port of Killala, inside Ireland's elbow. This was a trip which would teach me a number of lessons. Firstly, a lot of Irish anchorages are pretty tidal, secondly, the fishermen round here really are extraordinarily helpful, thirdly, the forecast for the swell is as important as the wind forecast and fourthly, never trust a South African hippy.

I motorsailed out of Sligo without running aground this time, in the wake of the yacht from Preston. With the north west wind gusting twenty five knots true I continued motorsailing into it all day until I was able to bear away a little after about thirty miles into the bay in which Killala sits. Like many Irish anchorages Killala is in a river estuary with something of a bar and often strong tides. Once over the bar there's a sheltered pool in which you can anchor tide rode. The fishing harbour is up a narrow marked channel between old training walls.

The South African hippy had assured me absolutely categorically, with his fantastic local knowledge, that I could pass over the bar into the sheltered pool at any state of tide. I would however have to wait until over half tide to get into the harbour, where I would remain afloat. After seven hours at sea I approached the bar just after low tide and could clearly see waves breaking over it. I went as close as I dared and decided there was no bleeding way I was taking the drug crazed lunatic's advice. I went and anchored outside the bar in an area of sea slightly sheltered by submerged rocks but still with a metre or so of swell off a lee shore, to wait for the tide and take stock, all the while cursing myself for listening to the loony.

The pilot book offered no numbers for a Harbourmaster or anyone else at Killala, but did list the number of a bloke who could give pilotage advice for the next estuary along. It was a bit of a long shot but I gave him a bell. His wife answered and had, understandably, some difficulty working out what I was on about. She gave me his mobile number, which he wasn't answering. A while later, as dusk approached, he phoned me back, having spotted that someone had phoned. I explained that I was at Killala, not 'his' estuary, and asked for advice on when I could enter. He told me in no uncertain terms that no-one had been able to enter or leave the estuary all day, that the swell would continue to break over the bar and that I'd be mad to attempt it. Oh shit. It was getting dark, I was alone and there were no safe havens within about seven hours. He asked me where I intended to go once across the bar. I said the harbour. He asked what harbour. I said "Killala". He said "but that's an entirely different estuary, I don't know anything about getting in there". It was with some relief that I told him he was a numbskull and I'd already explained which estuary I was at.

He then gave me the number of an old fisherman who keeps a lobster boat in Killala, Jimmy Gallagher. I had even more difficulty explaining to Jimmy what I wanted, but eventually he said that I could probably get over the bar at about ten p.m, but that the pool inside wasn't much of an anchorage and there was nowhere free inside the harbour where I could remain afloat. I thanked him and went back to cooking dinner while I waited for ten p.m. Much later than that and it might be difficult to negotiate my way up the unlit channel in the dark.

At nine p.m. my phone rang. It was Jimmy Gallagher. "Is that you anchored in the bay? I've driven over, moved my boat, climbed a hill and can see you with my binoculars. The swell has stopped breaking over the bar. You should be OK to cross it and enter the harbour if you're careful." Thanking him profusely I hauled up the anchor and headed in. On either side of me the waves broke and turned to white surf only a boat's length or two away, but in the middle of the channel they just steepened and we surfed down them. I was glad that Zoph is a directionally stable long keeler with a dirty great rudder. More modern boats might have been broached by the steep waves and sent in sideways.

A wave catching up with Zoph as she surfed over the bar into Killala

I followed the complex set of three pairs of white painted leading marks into the estuary. As I came abeam of the narrow channel to starboard into the harbour I had difficulty identifying which side of the withies to go. The phone rang again. It was Jimmy Gallagher. "You've just gone about twenty yards too far". Jimmy took my lines as I entered the harbour. Again I had difficulty with the strong tidal flow right up to the wall in the small fishing port. I rafted up on two other boats in his usual space, which he'd cleared for me.

He reckoned I'd have about a metre of water at low tide and should just sit upright in the mud and so it proved. We were on the bottom and heeled enough at four a.m. to wake me briefly, but not disastrously so. Jimmy explained that round here they use MagicSeaweed.com a lot, a surfing website which gives predictions of wave height and period, which they swear by. Swell height and steepness is more crucial than the wind forecast for getting over tidal bars on this exposed coast. Jimmy Gallagher wouldn't even take a beer for all his trouble. What a star.

Killala was a twee place with, as is traditional in that part of the world, about half as many pubs as houses. Wandering into one at random (a pub, not a house) I stumbled across an impromptu live music session. Four musicians of varying ages produced fiddles and guitars and blasted out some traditional tunes with great verve and skill. This session wasn't, as many are, for the tourists and seemed genuinely impromptu. It was encouraging to see quite young musicians carrying on this tradition.

Killala represented all the good and bad things about this coast. Really friendly people, loads of pubs with Guinness which really doesn't taste like the fizzy piss we get at home, twee villages, free berthing, horribly exposed coasts and strong tides running through anchorages.

My next stop, Broadhaven, it turned out, represented corporate greed and direct action against it by communities, but it didn't say that in the pilot book. The swell was still running as I headed over the bar at Killala on a rising tide just behind a friendly line-fishing trip boat with, it has to be said, a much shallower draught than Zoph. Leaving against the surf is, I was assured, much safer than arriving with it.

The breeze had gone round to the west, that is dead on the nose of course, so I motorsailed into eighteen to twenty two knot wind with two reefs in the main. The swell was still from the north west, making progress difficult even if I headed forty five degrees off the wind to seaward. I plugged away for a while to gain some sea room. Then I tacked several times to get round today's main obstacle, a group of rocks called The Stags. As I tacked through seventy degrees or so, with the waves against me the VMG on the GPS became negative on one tack. Eventually however I was able to ease the sheets and bear away a bit towards Broadhaven, where the pilot book promised visitors' moorings and a well fendered, sheltered pier.

I arrived in the bleak, wide inlet, exposed to northerly swells, to find no visitors' buoys and a steel piled pier conspicuously lacking in any soft bits and fully occupied by a couple of fishing boats at a time as they arrived to disgorge their catch then bugger off again. Apart from this activity, a deserted lifeboat station and two large black and yellow ribs marked 'Security Patrol' occupying two of the three private moorings, there was nobody and nothing to be seen. I asked one of the disgorging fishermen if the third mooring was likely to be occupied. He laughed bitterly and said he thought it unlikely.

The nearest settlement - and hence pub - was several miles away and I spent a lonely and rolly night getting generally hacked off at the seemingly endless series of wet batters to windward against big swells in the pissing down rain. Each day was spent in waking up, battering futilely to windward all day to somewhere which may or may not be accessible and secure, looking out the charts for the next day, having a beer and going to bed. This was meant to be fun and it was definitely beginning not to be. The prospect of another sixty mile trip the following day, round Erris Head and Achill Head, didn't help matters.

Though it's understandable that somewhere on the very tips of the fingers of Ireland should be bleak and uninhabited, the bleak, dead atmosphere of this place felt somehow intrinsically less welcoming than anywhere else in Ireland I'd been so far.

Much later, back at home, I caught a long, intense documentary on the telly about Broadhaven. It described the seething hatred of a small rural Irish community for Shell, who were trying to develop an oil field offshore and wanted to bring a pipeline ashore there. Unusually - and flying in the face of other documentary evidence such as 'Local Hero' - the entire community - not just some Eco hippies - was implacably, noisily and sometimes violently opposed to it. That night I had been sitting on one of the moorings which were all that was left of this conflict.

Later, in Galway, I met a couple of lads on a small scruffy yacht which, at the height of this conflict, had been boarded by private security thugs from ribs at sea, whilst perfectly innocently on passage near Broadhaven. I'd have been inclined to treat this act of piracy as a matter for the courts, but the lads seemed sanguine about it. Later, when they landed at Broadhaven they'd been totally ostrichised by the locals, who assumed they worked for Shell and buried their heads in sand.

Elsewhere in Ireland I started to spot quite a few old anti-shell posters and stickers, faded and peeling off lampposts. That's what the bent and gnarled fingers of Belmullet and Achill Island are doing; trying to stick two fingers up to Shell and the oilfields out to the west. My Dad, very much a company man who worked for Shell all his life, is doubtless spinning in his grave.

The next day I had a treat. An actual day of summer. It was bright and sunny, if cold at first, without a cloud in the sky. Little wind at all for a change, but Cheggers can't be boozers it seems and I wasn't complaining.

Achill Head

This was the first summer's day for eight days. Ireland wasn't getting too profligate with its summer weather however. This was to be the only day of summer allowed, followed the next day by force sevens from the south west. In a familiar pattern therefore I decided that I needed to use the good weather to put in some miles. I would nip round Erris Head and Belmullet, miss out the intriguingly named Blacksod Bay and pass round Achill Head - a massive rocky finger with some good tidal races around it - to South Achill Sound.

We motorsailed round Erris Head under main and engine, bore away and got a small push from the jib. The westerly swell was still running, but we passed inside Inishkea Islands and for once got a fairly calm sea for a bit before emerging and heading to keep a mile or so of the massive cliffs of Achill Head. As we rounded the head the swell fell away a bit and it suddenly felt like we were in sheltered waters, away from the wilds of the North Atlantic.

A quick look at the chart confirms that this bit of coast, even inside Achill Head, is about the most exposed in Europe, still entirely open to the south west. Virtually nowhere I've sailed in Scotland is as exposed to the ocean. But you get used to it and four miles in from Achill Head seemed for the moment like sheltered inland waters.

South Achill Sound was a very pictureskew - if extremely tidal - inlet. Theoretically you can pass right through it, using the new swing bridge, inside Achill Island and avoid the need to round Achill Head. A trip by Brompton bike later confirmed the existence of a new swing bridge allowing the passage. But there's virtually no information on this passage, in the pilot book or anywhere else I could find. Euromillions have built the swanky new bridge, along with a whole pile of other public works in the one horse village, but nobody ever uses it because they don't tell you how.

The pilot book was both dire and bollockal in other respects about Achill Sound. Various of the published phone numbers were wrong and it makes the entrance and anchorage sound very difficult, which they aren't, especially if you get the tide going the right way which, for once, I did. I picked up one of three brand new visitors' buoys laid by the Council. The other two were of course empty.

As the wind increased the following day I realised the downside of these nice secure moorings. With the tide running at up to 2.5 knots the 27 knots of wind was blowing entirely on the beam. This meant that Zoph was effectively motoring all night at 2.5 knots through a disturbed and choppy sea with a heel of about fifteen degrees. Halfway through the night the tide turned, as did Zoph. She heeled fifteen degrees the other way and deposited me out of bed.

This didn't really matter as I wasn't sleeping much anyway. I was listening to the waves slapping and the lines snatching and chafing. In these circumstances I suffer from being woken up suddenly by self-induced quiet. I know that if the waves are slapping and the lines are snatching she's still attached to the mooring. If all goes quiet there's something to worry about. But as I drift off to sleep the world naturally goes quiet - after all you can't hear stuff in your sleep. So what's left of my conscious brain immediately snaps me back awake until I can hear all the noises again. This is obviously a continuous - and very annoying - feedback loop of eternal stupid wakefulness.

Getting ashore proved difficult as well, but there were pubs to be gone to so I managed to row ashore with difficulty and the bike. On the way I spend half an hour or so trying to disentangle the lines to the buoy (like most west of Scotland visitors' moorings there were no pickups), which had been twisted out of all recognition by the changing tide and wind. The village was about four miles away, but I'm dedicated and not to be put off by mere distance.

On the way was a bleak, near deserted pub with a couple of neds and a pool table, and the local parish church. In common with many in Ireland this latter was a corrugated iron shed, circa 1930. We in Scotland are used to churches making up a part of the historical built fabric and in a deeply catholic country it comes as a surprise to find that most of the churches are in fact relatively new. Not necessarily of corrugated iron but certainly not dating from the middle ages. It is of course a reminder that Ireland was a conquered country whose dominant religion was suppressed, often violently, for centuries. In Scotland we are used to having English influence considered as an invasion, but much more so than that of Scotland, the history of Ireland is genuinely that of a colony under naked imperialism.

Also like many other places in Ireland at least one of the pubs was a slick cliché machine designed to suck in American tourists and make them cry. One of the downsides of a summer in Ireland was the number of American tourists. It's a market that the Irish seem to have tapped much more successfully than the Scots.

In one of the pubs a band was assembled. Two crusty old blokes and a couple of young lads being trained in the tear-jerking trade. They churned out - very professionally - all the old favourites. The Black Velvet Band, The Wild Rover and a succession of songs about how they miss their old Mum now that they've arrived on Ellis Island and they'll probably never see the old country again. All these songs are dedicated to their old long-lost septuagenarian cousin Bob, newly arrived from Urinal Idaho with a piece of paper from a genealogy website. All the old wifeys take it in turns to dance with Bob who, with tears streaming down his face, buys everyone drinks all night. It seems to be a successful business model.

The next day another British boat picked up one of the moorings. She was a small yawl called *'Hippo'* and sailed in with the wind still blowing force six and a gale in the forecast. All very intrepid. But in fact they've just launched her in nearby Rosmoney, having trailed her from somewhere in the south of Englandshire. Not a bad way of cruising this coast. Forget about all the bloody headlands and Bleedin' Forelands and just explore the indented bits in between, going by road from loch to loch.

Into Ireland's Oxter

After two nights the forecast improved and I left Achill Sound heading possibly for the harbour on Inishbofin and possibly for the mainland harbour of Clifden. This is a deeply indented coast with, for once, quite a number of off-lying islands to take shelter behind as I sailed south south west. With twelve to seventeen knots of breeze I sailed on a broad reach to the shelter of Clare Island, where I hardened up to a fine reach in the lee of the island. The pattern continued as I sailed round Inishturk, Inishbofin and a number of minor islets. I was able to bear away to a beam reach in the swell and harden up to a fine reach in the shelter. In this way I kept to nearly hull speed for some thirty miles. Albeit Zoph's hull speed is only about 6.4 knots. To cap it all it was actually sunny, with barely a cloud in the sky. A good sailing day for once and the best sail I'd had in Ireland so far.

Given these conditions I decided, inevitably, to miss out all the local goodies and head straight round Slyne Head and south east to Craggy Island. Since the north west wind was due to back westerly later who knew? Perhaps the fates might conspire to keep me sailing all day. I had to bear away a bit too much as I approach Slyne Head and the speed slowed, but I was still making over five knots over a blue sea in the sunshine.

At one point, down below making a cup of coffee, I heard a very high whistling noise. With the usual paranoia associated with any odd noises I suspected some problem with the engine. I shot up on deck to find we were being escorted by a big pod of dolphins. Of the smaller, Welsh or Bristol Channolean variety rather than the big Scottish east coast bottlenose ones. They stayed and played around in the bow wave for twenty minutes or so. I wasn't sure if I had imagined the whistle, but an hour or so later I heard it again, looked up and there they were again.

South Achill Sound

On the way to Slyne Head an old 13m wooden cutter called *'Mortvan'* passed me going north. This was the only proper cruising yacht I'd seen for eight days except for the Preston yacht in Sligo. One other yacht in over a week. After Slyne Head the motor went on and the staysail came down - it's useless on a run as it just takes the jib's wind - for the twenty mile final leg to Craggy Island. Ten miles after Slyne Head another yacht! A wee Hallberg Rassy with poorly set sails heading west. Blimey, it's getting like Piccadilly Circus round here.

The swell died away a bit as well as I headed east to Craggy Island, where I arrived just under twelve hours after leaving Achill Sound having covered sixty five miles and probably missed out half the highlights of the west of Ireland. The wide bay at Kilronan is reputed to have eight visitors' moorings and to be exposed to winds from the north and east. There's actually only four moorings, the others presumably having been removed to accommodate the massive new fifty million euro port development for the large number of fast ferries which transport thousands of tourists a day to this, Ireland's most visited tourist destination.

Only one of the buoys was free but I noticed a big Beneteau tied up against the gleaming white concrete wall in the brand spanking new, sheltered harbour. I asked if I could raft up on him and did so for the night. The Beneteau 41 was from Kilrush on the Shannon and the skipper was, of course, hugely friendly and accommodating to foreigners. Again and again he made me promise to look him up if I made it into the Shannon and again and again I said it was unlikely that I would enter the estuary.

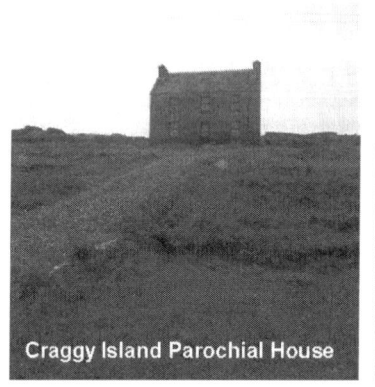

Craggy Island Parochial House

Genetically modified cows eat the rocks on Craggy Island

The following morning the Beneteau left and I moved Zoph into the corner of the harbour, away from the many ferries and few fishing boats and more sheltered from the waves bending through the entrance.

By day the harbour was a building site. Blokes in hard hats wielded JCBs and made a racket while Zoph sat inside the harbour in the usual building site exclusion zone behind fences and 'elf and safety signs warning of imminent death if you didn't wear a hard hat. That, the fact that it was a ferry berth and my experience of the swingeing exclusion zones in CalMac ports led me to worry about the presence of wee Zoph, moored for free against the wall. I needn't have worried. Only in Ireland do supervisors on building sites in hard hats march over to you just to ask, out of interest, where you are from and where you've been. The ferry crews just shrugged their shoulders and said I'd be fine where I was. Builders helped haul Bertie the Brompton Bike up the high harbour wall so that I could go for a cycle. Folk wandering by gave advice about my lines, which were unnecessarily complicated and eccentric as usual given the 4.5 metre spring tides. As before, the stand-out feature of cruising Ireland's west coast was the friendliness of the people.

Craggy Island, and its neighbour Rugged Island, are of course better known as the setting for Father Ted, for which series they are renamed Inishmore and Inishmaan, the Aran Islands. They are, stretching anatomical metaphors to breaking point, the belly-button fluff of Ireland. That is the only fluffy thing about them. In all other respects they are... well, craggy and rugged. Even cragged and ruggy

Every day it seems that several milliard touros, mostly on hired bikes, descend on Craggy Island. I would hesitate to call them cyclists. In fact I would not call them cyclists. Most of them seemed to have tremendous difficulty staying aboard their vehicles as they wobbled rotundly up the road. There was a distressingly large numbers of Americans on the island and as you can imagine those who had been cajoled onto bikes were amongst the least capable.

Of the tourists Americans seemed almost to be in the majority, but this is often the case and it is likely that it was just that they were making the majority of the noise. After Americans the largest group of foreign tourists was probably French, perhaps reflecting the direct ferry link from Brittany to Rosslare and the generally miserable reception they would get if they went to England. It also highlighted another connection within the Gaelic, or in this case possibly Garlic 'fringe' of Europe.

Staying a whole day on Craggy Island I joined the cycling hordes and Brompted down it. As is usually the case with the major tourist draws you only need to take a wrong turn for a few hundred yards and there's scarcely any of them left. Millions of people thronged around the main hill fort - the one you had to pay to get into. I visited another one as well – actually a shorter walk from the road and almost as intact – and there wasn't a single other person there.

The Craggy Island hill forts are quite striking, with their concentric circular dry stone walls. The one with all the touros is a semi-circle built right to the edge of a vertiginous cliff. The island rises in a gentle slope from north to south. The south side falling vertically to the sea. There is something a little suspicious about the hill forts. It seems to me there's little chance that dry stone constructions could have survived the claimed 3000 years as intact as they appear, in a landscape so harsh with a population so intent on building thousands of walls between fields. My guess would be that a large amount of strategic rebuilding has gone on to ensure the tourist income, without being too precious about the archaeology.

The rest of the landscape is quite striking as well. It can best be described by the word 'rocks'. It's not a particularly high island, but it is a rocky one. Almost surreally rocky. The land is divided into small fields entirely strewn with rocks. From any sort of distance it looks completely like the cows are just grazing on rock. It's not an entirely lovely island, especially compared to other landscapes on Ireland's west coast and considering how many touros it attracts, but it is a striking and somewhat weird one.

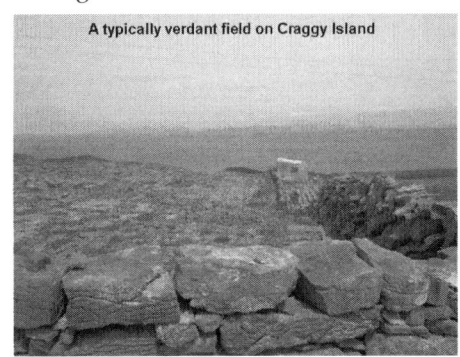

A typically verdant field on Craggy Island

The obvious harshness of the barren landscape is made more surreal by the fact that, in the Celtic tiger economy, there's obviously been plenty of money about, so the low hills are strewn, not only with rocks, but with more or less suburban bungalows of varied architectural styles and merit. These Irish rural communities are always a surprise to someone used to the west of Scotland. Whilst rural Ireland was severely affected by the potato famine in the 19th century, it retained a large and dispersed population which recovered. The villages are still there and round every headland there's another settlement. A lot of the landscape looks like the west of Scotland, but with people. Round a similar headland in Scotland and you are greeted by the sight of a couple of abandoned shielings and a few bits of broken down stone wall.

The clearances were what made the difference. Scotland was forcibly depopulated and has never recovered. I noticed the same phenomenon in Norway as in Ireland. There as well the rural population is scattered all the way up the coast. The whole of the western fringe of northern Europe, to beyond seventy degrees north, is littered with agricultural settlements with plenty of new development and small industry. Except the west of Scotland, about which we are routinely told that it's way too remote and barren to support anything. We can learn from elsewhere in the Celtic Fringe.

As elsewhere in Ireland there's obvious money, an apparently less prescriptive planning system than in Britain, which seems to allow very mixed architectural styles, and plenty of evidence of economic downturn. All along the coast of Ireland are expensive looking, small, spec-build developments which seem to have been cut off in their prime. Empty, almost complete houses with grass growing through the piles of abandoned building materials in the garden.

Not everyone biked to the hill forts. Aside from the bands of the suggestible in horse drawn traps, a school crocodile of about fifty teenage kids walked past. Presumably hiking the eight mile round trip on foot. Bringing up the rear was a girl on crutches. Well, I suppose what doesn't kill you will make you stronger. Most of the folk on bikes aren't exactly going to be competing in the Tour de France. I went faster than most of them on my knackered, rusting, single-geared folding Brompt and a lot of them walked up the slightest incline.

But in the bike park at the main fort one group stood out. They had a guide who was loudly ordering them about and had delineated an exclusive area for their preparation. They were donning day-glow jackets, on a bright sunny afternoon on an island with almost literally no traffic at all. As I stopped for photography a little later, on a deserted single track road with no traffic, they came by in procession. Each had a day-glow tabard, a cycling helmet and knee pads and each of their bikes, in the full light of the early afternoon June sun, had its headlight on. I'm not one for spreading racial stereotypes but if the helmet fits... I'm afraid to say that their guide was shouting at them in German. They were, of course, cycling Helmuts.

Local people seem to be remarkably sanguine and pragmatic about the fantastically negative image presented of Craggy Island in the Father Ted series. In it the island is portrayed as the arsehole of the universe, yet the locals seem to revel in it and the tourists flock in droves. An example of positive marketing generated from this negative imagery is the painting all over the window of the tea shop. I'm sure you can guess whose face peers out at you insisting that you partake in a cup of tea.

There's an annual 'Tedfest' filled with events such as Father Jack cocktail evenings, which involve the consumption of cleaning fluids, to which 2000 of the faithful flock. Apparently there's far too much demand for the local hotels and B&Bs and most Ted fans sleep in tents. It hardly needs to be said that Tedfest happens in February. The festival is so popular that competition to hold the various events is settled by a five a side football match between Craggy and Rugged Islands.

Craggy Island is a strange place. Ironically, not to say paradoxically, it looks arid. Almost like some of the places I've hiked about in Turkey. The thousands of roughly constructed walls surrounding nothing very much are even reminiscent, bizarrely, of Lanzarote. It's so rocky, with such poor and thin

A group of cycling Helmuts

soil, that it seems parched. Chiming with this image I saw a water Department 'Conservation and Leaks Van'. With the porous geology and no standing water I suspect potable water's a rare commodity, despite the fact that it always pisses down, which must be very annoying. Huge amounts of stone have been used to build ridiculous numbers of walls round fields some of which seem to have no soil at all. I suspect a lot of the walls are for wind reduction rather than to keep the cows in.

On my second night the weather turned a bit nastier. It pissed down and the breeze got up to about a force six. I spent quite a lot of time in and out of the pub, scaling the ladder down into the dark hole of the harbour at low tide and trying to leap onto Zoph as she surged back and forth about six feet from the wall, to adjust the lines.

Once again - and surprisingly given the fact that the local population is outnumbered by touros about 1000 to 1 - everyone was extraordinarily friendly. I twice got free ice from the pub to top up my fridge, which only really works when under motor or plugged into the mains. A mixed group of local fishermen and sailors at home on leave from small coasters got chatting to me in the pub. There was none of the usual antagonism towards yachties, just interest in where I'd been. One of them who, it must be said, was particularly pissed, bought me, unbidden, a pint of Guinness. Whilst grateful, my mean streak was worried that this was going to involve large rounds, cost me a lot and get me too pissed to climb down the ladder onto Zoph. But ten minutes later the pissed fisherman wandered off into the night. The pint was just a genuine act of friendliness.

For the first time in Ireland I had first hand evidence of Irish Gaelic - or 'Irish' as it is simply called - genuinely being spoken. Quite a number of the older folk spoke it. Elsewhere the evidence was only to be found in the street signs. If it's anything like Scotland this is no evidence at all. All the places on the Black Isle, near Inverness, for example, have been given pseudo-Gaelic names on the road signs. This despite the fact that nobody has spoken the language there for hundreds of years and the locals don't even know what the Gaelic name for their village is.

Presumably reflecting the fact that a few folk actually speak the language, some of the council's signs on Craggy Island are <u>only</u> in Irish, not in English at all. This included a couple of ridiculous road signs urging, I think, caution approaching a bend in the road. Since all the locals presumably already know that they need to exercise caution on their one public road and 99.99% of the people who use the road - the touros - don't speak a word of the language, one can only assume that the hazards are not so great that you actually need to know about them. The worst excesses of linguistic political correctness in Scotland can't compete with monolingual Gaelic signs.

After my second night in the belly button fluff it was time to head for the oxter - the armpit of Eire. I ought to have been heading south for the groinal area and the knees, but the forecast for the next few days looked predictably dire, with consistently strong south westerlies, so I decided to head for Galway. Just as I left Craggy Island a 'small craft warning' was issued on the VHF. This is for winds of force six and above, but they were south westerlies so would push me nicely to Galway. We sailed all the way under jib alone. The sea grew rolly once out of the lee of Craggy Island, but it's relatively sheltered up near the oxters. The early mist burned off to give sun and a steady twenty knots of wind, rising to twenty six knots as time went on.

There's a small municipal marina in the centre of Galway. It was the first marina, or indeed place where it was possible to leave a boat for more than a couple of hours, since the Northern Irish border, nearly four hundred miles away by Zoph. There's apparently a marina in the river Bann, near the border, But I'd not seen anywhere you could leave a boat since Ardfern, some 450 miles away.

Galway Marina is in the main harbour basin, right in the centre of town. It's accessed by lock gates and accessible from two hours before high water to high water. I'd timed my twenty six mile trip to arrive a bit early for the locking and there appeared already to be a boat waiting. A large Jeanneau sitting on an incredibly uncomfortable mooring out in the bay, at the mercy of the waves and the chop and what remained of the swell sweeping in from the Atlantic. I confidently expected it to follow me into the harbour. A week later the Jeanneau was still there. Apparently it's a RYA training yacht operated, presumably, by a sado-masochist.

The lock opened twenty minutes early, just as I was approaching, so I entered and tied to a nice wee pontoon, surrounded by other yachts, including the friendly Beneteau from Craggy Island, in absolute, perfect shelter on a flat piece of water on which not a ripple could be seen. I'd not exactly had it rough up to that point, but it did make me realise how nice perfectly sheltered marina berths can be.

Galway was by far the largest town I'd been to in Ireland so far and it was a pleasant place to wander round. A University town it had something of a cosmopolitan atmosphere. It also had a lot of touros. Presumably mostly on the way to or from Craggy Island. A couple of the streets had a Mediterranean feel, with restaurants spilling tables out onto the street and waiters touting for trade. A number of the pubs advertised live music and this really was aimed at making the American tourists cry. All very fake but quite pleasant nonetheless.

Since the weather didn't look like it was going to improve for the foreseeable I decided to go home for a few days and leave Zoph at Galway. With the help of the usual friendly locals I'd arranged for a mechanic to take a look at the engine, which had been steaming a little worryingly since we left Port Ed. The diagnosis was salt build-up in the raw water intake blocking the flow. Not too serious but it could do with being looked at.

I flew to Edinburgh out of the bizarre Knock Airport. Sitting in a field in the middle of nowhere it mostly takes the great unwashed of Ireland to Ibitha on Ryan Air. It was originally built to bring in pilgrims to visit 'Knock Shrine'. This is the site of an apparent 'apparition', where various people in the 19th century, probably off their faces on laudanum, saw the images of what looked like biblical types on a rock. The airport itself is of course described on various plaques and information boards as a miracle and is the only Ryan Air destination thought to have been actually sanctioned and funded by God. Reading the nonsense on posters at the airport about the miracle of Knock Airport I felt as though I'd wandered out of reality and into a Father Ted script.

Typically lovely summer weather on passage

Belly Button and Legs

I returned five days later and was joined by another chum from Port Edgar, Fiona Harrison. Fiona and her husband Simon sail a Sadler 32 called 'Moonwhite'. I also joined her for part of her trip round England and Wales aboard her Albin Vega, 'Dumbea'. Fiona is therefore the only person I know of, outside the immediate descendents of Walt Disney, who owns two yachts both named after characters out of Disney cartoons, 'Snow White' and 'Dumbo'.

I was glad to have crew for the next bit since the long passages, battering into the swell and wind, were beginning to get me down a bit. Zoph's wind vane self-steering and tillerpilot work well and it's usually possible to do stuff other than helming whilst on passage single-handed. But when the boat's bucking around like billy o and the waves are big you've pretty much got to be near the helm all day. This made some of the eight to twelve hour passages somewhat wearing and the prospect of having crew was reassuring. The sight of Fiona's fiddle emerging from its wrapping (she'd actually had it sent by post to Galway so that she could practice every day on board) was rather less encouraging.

We left as the lock gates opened at 8.30 am heading, unfortunately, back to Craggy Island, Galway having been something of a side detour. We left without having been able to pay the mechanic for his apparently stirling work de-scaling the engine, but he was Irish so on the phone he didn't seem too bothered by this and said he'd send a bill somewhere, sometime. The plan was to catch the ebb tide down to Craggy before the west north west wind increased from force three to force six, which it was predicted to do later in the day.

For two hours we motorsailed into the fairly gentle wind then suddenly, out of nowhere, there was a loud bang, a massive plume of black smoke erupted from the exhaust and the engine started racing madly. I scrabbled for the key to turn the engine off at the companionway but it kept on racing. As I turned the key Fiona put the engine in neutral and eventually it responded to being turned off at the key. Oh shit. What to do now? There was obviously some serious problem with the engine. The fact that a mechanic had just been tinkering with it couldn't be ignored.

We set sail back to Galway while I phoned the mechanic who agreed to meet us at the quayside, in a little cut outside the lock gates which didn't dry. The lock gates would have long been shut as the tide fell. I also phoned Bukh UK in Poole. Neither the mechanic nor Bukh could come up with any plausible hypothesis as to what had happened. Needless to say the engine worked fine to get us back into Galway, where we met the mechanic. There was a slightly embarrassing moment when I mistook the guy, who I'd never met, for a local fisherman just friendly enough to rush about helping with our lines. All he or

Bukh could suggest was that we went out and motored around rapidly, with him on board, seeking a recurrence of the problem. This we did and of course the engine has never operated so smoothly.

We thanked him, paid him for his previous work and headed back out to sea at one p.m. By now, of course, we had exhausted most of the ebb and the wind, right on the nose, was rising. Unsure of the engine we avoided motorsailing and sailed on a dead beat all the way to Craggy with two reefs in the main and the wind on the nose and increasing to force six. We made it at around nine p.m. having taken twelve hours and travelled fifty four miles to cover a straight line distance of twenty six miles. Just for the record, the things that broke or in some way failed during that passage were: The engine (temporarily), the anemometer, the GPS, a reefing line, the staysail halyard and the cockpit table.

Giving Loop Head a wide berth

Much later, reflecting on our mechanical problems, I came up with a rather prosaic hypothesis which I am increasingly convinced explains all the symptoms. I believe that a member of the crew, who shall be nameless, unbeknownst to her/him, sat vigorously, suddenly and heavily on the throttle, pushing it all the way down very rapidly to a point it had never been pushed before and causing a loud noise, a huge belch of black smoke and a racing engine. A minute later that same crew member, on request, put the throttle into neutral so that there was no evidence of the misdemeanour. This would explain why all returned to normal so rapidly. But surely two relatively experienced sailors couldn't have called out a mechanic, bothered the manufacturer and interrupted a passage for something so pedestrian and trivial... could they? I'll leave you to judge.

Another night passed uneventfully tied to the harbour wall at Craggy Island, though sensitive eared locals passing nearby may have discerned what sounded like cats being tortured at the bottom of the wall. Fiona's fiddle was out of its wrapping.

The next leg was a necessarily long one. From Craggy Island to Loop Head and the Shannon estuary the cliffs stretch south west unbroken for forty-odd miles. The minimum passage distance to a safe haven is almost sixty miles and there's little point in going into the very tidal Shannon as you just need to plug out of it again against the tide. We were therefore heading for Fenit, a marina in Tralee Bay in County Kerry on an odd little island with a causeway and bridge to the mainland.

Whilst I was home in Edinburgh from Galway Dave Punton - he of the Sigma 33 *'Kittiwake'* fame - had, with apparent kindness, lent me Roger Oliver's strangely pedantic and detailed book about circumnavigating mainland Britain and Ireland. Roger's circumnavigation was a proper one, not involving any canals.

Dave is of course an accomplished sadist and had mostly given me the book to draw my attention to Oliver's account of trying to get from Fenit to Craggy Island. It's the most scary passage in the book. In it he leaves Fenit to cross the entrance to the Shannon in a force five, on an ebb tide when there had been a south westerly gale blowing a couple of days earlier. Within a few miles he is down to bare poles and his boat is being flattened by each wave. In attempting to turn back to Fenit he manages to break several fingers, mash up his face and destroy his groinal area on a winch. Dave, pissed off at having to stay at home and work instead of going sailing, titters with glee as I read the passage with increasingly alarm.

With the forecast for force three to five north west, backing west, we headed out of Craggy Island and between it and Rugged Island under full sail. Mindful of the dire warnings about the ebb tide in the Shannon I set a course to pass in a curve way out to the west, avoiding the tide and the possibility of being headed by the backing wind. It's amazing, if you are me, how rare it is to set a direct straight line course. There's always a reason to go in a curve and this time both the Shannon tides and the backing winds suggested a westwards curve.

It was one of the best sails of the summer. Under full sail we turned off the engine within a hundred yards of the harbour entrance and didn't turn it on again until a hundred yards from the harbour entrance at Fenit, over sixty miles later. In full sun and with relatively little swell we sailed on a reach at between 4.5 and 6.5 knots for eleven hours.

One larger yacht, a Westerly Storm named *'Scaraveen'* overtook us on the way down, also heading for Fenit but taking a much more direct, coastal course past Loop Head. Sod's law dictated that, having seen bugger-all boats for a fortnight, now that we were heading for places with more yacht traffic our arrival at Fenit should coincide with the entire racing fleet of about twenty yachts all suddenly coming out in the opposite direction under full sail. It almost made me nostalgic for Port Edgar.

The welcome at the marina didn't. Having phoned ahead we were told, not that we couldn't expect to turn up without being on a waiting list, but that we'd be welcome. Though we were approaching more yachtie territory and having to pay for berthing again, at least they were friendly. A marina manny phoned us up repeatedly asking exactly when we would arrive so that he could show us to a berth, take our lines, give us gate codes and generally make us feel welcome. The contrast between this and a visitor's arrival at surly old Port Edgar was a stark one.

Fiona was less than impressed that the marina manny called us 'lads' all the time, but subsequent observations suggest that this may be an Irish term which has acquired similar generic connotations to the term 'guys'. This latter is now applied to groups of people regardless of sex by young waiting staff and others in Britain. I suspect that, to an Irish marina manny the term 'lads' applied to a woman is seen as complimentary, implying the proper crew status often not accorded to girlies.

The first boats for weeks and it's a whole racing fleet heading for us

A mad statue of St Brendan the Navigator in Fenit. He is supposed to have 'discovered' America 800 years before Columbus

We were, of course, made to pay for our one great summer sailing day with two conspicuously crap ones and three nights stuck in Fenit marina. On the positive side we were perfectly comfortable. The marina manny had ensured that Zoph was facing bow to the south westerly gales that lashed the marina, whose waters were well sheltered, but whose little island was entirely exposed to the storm. I employed Zoph's new all over cockpit tent, which keeps at least some of the rain out at the expense of ruining her rather nice lines. On the negative side snatches of the sound of cats being tortured coming from Zoph were whipped away on the wind as I prowled the pontoons and surrounding docks in the rain.

A large mob-handed German yacht called in at Fenit briefly. About a fifty foot Beneteau or Bavaria circumnavigating Ireland as part of a mile-building course. Their last stop before Fenit had been Bangor in Belfast Lough. This is almost exactly at the opposite end of Ireland. I know I'd missed out a lot of good places whilst trying to escape the weather, but I do wonder what the point is in sailing all the way round a country hardly stopping at all. They spent the night, refuelled and headed out again into the teeth of the gale. I'm not sure what the next stop was to be. Hamburg or somewhere I'd imagine.

Walking across the causeway we noticed a bloke outside a camper van with a Welsh number plate. He was fishing off the causeway. For three days he sat in the rain and the wind on this unattractive concrete causeway in an unremarkable corner of Ireland dangling his hook. He was fishing from before nine in the morning until at least eleven at night. On the third day we asked him if he'd caught anything since he'd been there. "Not a single thing" he answered. They're a strange breed, anglers.

The bar in the rather nice sailing club building, with its panoramic views over the mountains to the south, was a predictably friendly place where even the racing sailors were keen to chat to us about where we had been. Hopefully they weren't drummed out of the Racing Union afterwards for talking for mere cruisers. Skaraveen's skipper offered us a lift into the nearby town of Tralee, which we gratefully accepted. We had a pleasant day wandering the streets of another very pleasant county town which I had vaguely heard of but couldn't place on the map.

The only reference I could dig out of my brain to Tralee was a vague recollection that there was a song called 'The Rose of Tralee'. True to form the locals run an old fashioned beauty pageant on the basis of the song and market this aberration as an international festival. Instituted in 1959 it should probably have stayed in the 1950s.

We subjected ourselves to several hours in the local museum, which was extremely instructive, giving a potted Irish history from about 8000 years ago to the day before yesterday. It really is embarrassing how little I knew about Irish history. It's just the next bit of land to the west and its history has been inextricably linked to that of Scotland, England and the UK. Just about every event described at Tralee had something to do with the English and/or the Scots and I knew next to nothing about any of it.

Do you know when Ireland became a republic, for example? Well done if you said 1949. After World War Two! I'd have sworn it was about thirty years earlier than that. It had all sorts of different statuses before that, but wasn't actually a republic until then. I told myself that my shameful ignorance wasn't that unusual and was shared by most Brits.

The Irish, on the other hand pretty much know everything that happens in the UK. In a way they have no choice. As in Scotland, a lot of the pubs show Sky telly on big screens. When the news comes on, it's all from London and deals in British news almost exclusively. It's annoying enough for us in Scotland to be bombarded by a Londoncentric media, but when it happens in an entirely independent country which fought and struggled to gain that independence for generations, it must be especially galling. Since we stopped using the seas as our main highways and started using the land, the air and, in the case of satellite telly, outer space, the whole of the Celtic Fringe is now on a long lead from the land of the Angles.

Fenit, Ireland's kneecap, wasn't unpleasant but neither did it have a great deal to recommend it as anything other than a port in a storm. So we were glad to be heading onwards after three nights listening to the gales. The day we left the wind started in the south at around force six but was due to decrease and veer west then increase again and veer north. We were heading west to Sybil Point, then south inside the Blasket Islands, then either east to Dingle or South east to Valentia. So there was about one chance in a million that the wind would shift at exactly the right time and allow us to sail on a reach all the way.

As we headed off downwind behind Scaraveen, which was heading for Dingle for a day or two, the sun disappeared and we sped along in squalls with about 25 knots of true wind behind us. Several other local boats were also out but they soon turned back and Scaraveen went on ahead. As the weather worsened the wind dropped and after a while we were motorsailing. Scaraveen called us on the radio from a couple of miles ahead and said the wind had gone westerly and that they were giving up and returning to Fenit rather than fight the wind and waves. Brilliant. Were they saying that the wind and waves were getting higher and making for a difficult passage, or just that they couldn't be arsed motoring into them? I had difficulty getting a satisfactory answer. As usual however, Zoph was heading for the next big headland alone.

In the event the one in a million chance almost paid off and we passed Sybil point and headed south inside the toenails of the Blaskets just as the wind went north north west and increased to a good solid force four. We sailed on a broad reach past Dunmore Head, Ireland's big toe and reached Zoph's most westerly point ever at ten and a half degrees. Since her most easterly point so far is Orust Island in Sweden at fifteen degrees, that's about a fifteenth of the way round the world. Not very impressive. Could do better.

Once again the short-lived good conditions proved the curse of the cruising sailor. We could have gone into Dingle, which seems generally to be recommended by everyone I've spoken to. But again we missed out a fertile cruising ground because we wanted to put in plenty of mileage after being stuck for three nights in Fenit. I was also mindful of the need to deposit Fiona somewhere sensible, with public transport, at the end of her week. So we carried on southwards, extending the passage to fifty miles, outside Valentia Island for the sheltered inlet of Port Magee.

The Westerly Storm 'Scaraveen'... or part of her at least

Entering this beautiful inlet we passed very quickly from exposed ocean swell to perfect shelter. As is often the case on the west of Ireland, seen from the sea there appeared to be only rocks and cliffs, with no obvious entrance and certainly no settlement. As we entered between the rocks the landscape soon softened to a more agricultural one and out of nowhere farms and a village appeared. The land behind the facade of cliffs is not, as on the west of Scotland, more and more wild and mountainous, but more and more pastoral and gentle.

We followed quite a tortuous channel to several visitors' buoys near the head of the inlet, before it is blocked by a low bridge over to Valentia Island. There was one other boat on the moorings, a large British Oyster cruising the south coast. We were beginning to enter the areas where people actually go cruising. Unfortunately the moorings were on the opposite side of the inlet to the pictureskew, multicoloured village, which was a good long row away.

Fiona had long expressed the desire to find some traditional music in pubs, but attempts to land on the nearer shore and walk round via the bridge proved difficult, so Fiona stayed on board torturing cats while I undertook the long row in search of a pint. It was Sunday night at 10.30 and the little village looked quiet so I suspected the best I could hope for was a quick pint in a deserted pub just before chucking-out time.

Organising the watch. In these conditions a good skipper will piss off down below as soon as he's snapped the photo

Near Mizen Head

Portmagee has about fifty houses and, in a ratio common in rural Ireland, about seventeen pubs. That Sunday night they were mostly absolutely hooching. At least two of them had live music with local folk bands blasting out all the favourites for the hundreds of tourists, both Irish and foreign, who rammed the place. By midnight there was absolutely no sign of proceedings winding up but I thought I'd better head back, while I could still row and before Fiona put out a MOB Mayday. Suffice to say I was smug about my live pub music experience.

There's certainly life in the Irish pub yet. Many of them have not seen the need to install big screen tellies, most of them are still open and plenty of them seem to be doing good business, at least in summer, despite smoking bans. And I can confidently report that it's not due to the paltry price of the beer, which isn't.

Having passed our most westerly point there was a real sense that we'd broken the back of the Irish west coast as we headed out next morning for Dursey Head and Mizen Head. Once again we were missing out the deeply indented and fertile cruising grounds, this time Bantry Bay and Dunmanus Bay, in order to put some miles in, in this case again about fifty. The northerly wind rose from ten to eighteen knots and we motorsailed downwind under the main, unfurling the jib at Dursey Head as we turned to bring the wind on the port quarter. Three yachts passed us going in the opposite direction. Some dolphins joined us for a wee gambol for a few minutes. Piccadilly bloody circus. As we rounded Mizen Head we hardened up, the engine was turned off and we sailed up Ireland's foot.

Although on the face of it the south coast of Ireland is just as exposed to the prevailing south westerlies as the west, there seems to be an awful lot less swell in the south and as soon as we passed Mizen Head this became obvious as the waves fell away a bit. This trend was to continue as we passed other milestones along the coast. It's still a pretty exposed bit of sea and potentially very rough, but there's a definite falling away in the size of the seas as you move from west to south.

Our destination that evening was Crookhaven and we eventually beat into the narrow, east facing inlet as the wind went to the west. In Crookhaven, underlining the fact that we had more or less turned the corner onto the south coast, there were about fifteen visitors' moorings, though almost all of them were empty. Again underlining the fact that we were no longer on the west coast, we had to pay for the rather dodgy looking mooring at the local shop. The first mooring I'd paid for since Ardfern. I'd only gone into the shop to ask if the moorings were properly maintained. Instead of giving me any sort of answer, the girl just routinely produced a receipt book and demanded money. Definitely a sea change in the economics of cruising, as well as a sea change in the sea.

Crookhaven

We ate ashore that night in the attractive and fairly well touristed village, then did a very minor pub crawl of two pubs. I spoke to an elderly chap sporting an impressive moustache and a tee shirt proclaiming a round Britain and Ireland sailing cruise. The shirt was printed with the ports of call which included Orkney and showed that he'd actually done a proper circumnavigation of the mainland. As I congratulated him on this Fiona propounded the outrageous view that a trip round the southern half of Britain, via the Forth-Clyde canal, constituted a "circumnavigation of Britain by the lowland route". Excited, I rushed to join the British Olympic team and I now hope to beat Usain Bolt in the 200m by running the shorter, 'lowland 200m', which is actually only 100m. I can't wait.

The sailing was definitely getting easier and the next day we had a great sail under full sail and full sun, with a nice gentle westerly pushing us along on a couple of broad reaches. We passed north of the Fastnet Rock and south of Cape Clear, reaching Zoph's most southerly point this year at about 51º 24' North. We watched a helicopter landing atop the Fastnet and leaving again as we relaxed in the sun. It wasn't just that the weather was nice or that we were now running with the waves, the whole nature of the sea on the south coast felt entirely different to the west.

Annoyingly, the peace was shattered by a fast rib, accompanied at a distance by its mother ship, a sinister looking grey painted customs ship. Three black-clad customs officers were in the rib.

It always seems odd that customs, border control and the police are the only people who wear black waterproofs. The rest of us sail mostly in good conditions in the daylight and don't do a lot of jumping off our boats. We are exhorted to wear brightly coloured waterproofs covered in day-glow patches, because obviously you can't be seen if you are floating about in dark coloured gear. Customs, border patrols and the police routinely travel about in ribs in the dark and in rough seas, boarding boats whose crews sometimes don't want to be boarded. They always wear black waterproofs and tackety black boots, minimising the chances of them being able to survive a fall into the sea. Why do they do this? I think it's just because they think they look cooler and more menacing in black. Remember, after all, that they are just lads and they do watch Hollywood films.

Leaving Crookhaven

Our Men in Black - actually two men and a woman - rammed Zoph alongside with the black rubber rubbing strake of their rib. They weaved about to thwart my attempts to introduce a fender between their black bits and Zoph's hull. Two of them came on board and spent ten minutes or so filling in forms in the sun. They were perfectly friendly and gave us quantities of tourist advice about Cork, then buggered off without any serious searching. God knows why they bothered. We were rounding the south western corner of Ireland and blindingly obviously not coming from a foreign country. Presumably they have quotas of foreign vessels to meet, small yachts are much easier to board than big ships, and it was a nice day for a quick boarding.

The yacht traffic was still increasing and we caught up with a black Westerly Centaur heading the same way as us. The photo of our destination, Glandore Harbour, in the pilot book, showed a black Westerly Centaur on a mooring, so we sort of followed him on the basis that must have been where he was going, and so it proved. The rocks on the way into the harbour are rather pedantically named 'Outer Danger, Middle Danger, Inner Danger and Sunk Rock'. It was like being in Australia with their imaginatively named 'Great Sandy Desert', which is a big sandy desert, and 'Great barrier Reef', which is a big barrier reef.

Glandore Harbour is a lovely estuarine inlet with two villages, Glandore and Union Hall, on opposite sides of it. We plumped for Glandore, with its hyper-posh houses lining the bay and about four pubs in a row. There were fewer visitors' moorings than advertised however. We could only see two amongst the many moorings for local boats, but picked up one of them. It is rumoured that the bloke who collects money for these moorings has no particular right to, but is just a chancer. Happily he didn't show so I didn't have to call his bluff.

Racing past the Fastnet

Glandore Harbour

The atmosphere was that of holidays and high summer, with various sprogs swimming about and the more spoilt ones razzing about in daddy's rib by themselves. We tackled all four of the pubs in a minor crawl. The landlady of one told us that, though there was obviously plenty of money about and it was more or less within commuting distance of Cork, the place was absolutely dead in the winter. A pity, since it was an attractive place. There were rocky inlets like the west of Scotland, with pastoral land behind, much more verdant green growth along the cliffs than we would expect in Scotland and the mansions of the rich lining the inlet. As regards the mansions, the Irish could really do with some access legislation like the Scots. There's a frustrating number of keep out signs preventing access to places which we would have the legal right to get to.

The conditions remained pretty good the following day, with enough wind so that we cansail to Kinsale. We started in full sun and a nice moderate breeze but inevitably the wind rose steadily, the sun disappeared and a series of rain squalls hit us. The aim when skippering in rain showers is to time watches so that the crew is steering when the squalls hit and you can disappear down below, perhaps offering to put on the kettle as a smokescreen for your real motive. The trick is to organise periods of helming casually and in a way that disguises your true motive of staying dry.

With the wind over twenty knots we sailed down wind under main only, with a boom preventer of course. As it dropped we unfurled the jib and made 4.5 to 5.5 knots most of the way to Kinsale. As the wind dropped further boat speed dropped to three to four knots. On previous passages we couldn't have afforded to sail so slowly. When you've got to make sixty miles in a day you want to be averaging five knots and this often leads to more motoring than you might want. On passages of thirty to thirty five miles however, leisurely sailing is more likely to be possible and this makes for much more relaxed cruising. This cruising was made the more laid back by the landscape, which softened progressively as we passed further east, from the dramatic, seemingly impregnable sea cliffs of the west to a quintessentially Irish, Kerrygold advert of rolling, green, pastoral fields.

Having dropped, the wind increased again as we approached the river and we motored into Kinsale harbour. Now we were really in the heart of Irish sailing country and it felt to some extent like the end of an adventure. I was actually almost as far away from home as I'd get this year, but I had broken the back of the trip and was back in nice friendly cruising grounds. There's three marinas in Kinsale, more than on the whole west and north coasts of Ireland. We plumped for the Kinsale Yacht Club marina and tied to an outer pontoon, a bit subject to the wash of passing boats, behind a huge posh Dutch motor barge.

Dolphins joined us for a gambol but were less than photogenic

Behind Ireland's Knees

Kinsale is probably Ireland's poshest place and it shows in the prices, from the marina costs (€27 a night for an eight metre boat and €2 for a cold shower in this theoretically not-for-profit marina) to the restaurants for which the town is apparently well known. The folk in the club were friendly enough, though with a bit more posh urban reserve than I'd been used to elsewhere. It's certainly a fairly swanky club where you book for dinner and the wood panelled walls are lined with trophies and pictures of past Commodores. The pilot book says that the marina fees buy you "temporary membership". A suggestion refuted by the signs to the showers which say "Visitors Showers" and "Members only, no visitors beyond this point". I wonder if the members get hot showers.

There had recently been some shenanigans at Port Edgar, where the local council had decided to stop running the marina because it was a popular facility and a financial success. Various groups had therefore been looking at the possibility of taking it over and running it as a not for profit enterprise. Fiona was therefore interested in the fact that the Kinsale club owns and runs its own marina. She sought out the powers that be to pick their brains and soon we were surrounded in the bar by a bevy of Commodores, Honorary Treasurers and the like.

Kinsale Yacht Club Marina

To my mind the problem of having a community resource owned and run by a yacht club, as opposed to a wider community group, was perfectly illustrated by the Commodore's answer to a question of mine. Interested in the mix of boats and keen to explore how a marina can be a genuine community resource I said "I see you also have small motorboats and workboats in the marina...". "Ah yes, them", interrupted the Commodore rather wearily, "We're forced to have them because some of our shallow draught moorings aren't suitable for yachts. We'd get rid of them all if only we could dredge all the moorings". He was evidently affronted by small scruffy boats that didn't have masts or race. He assumed that I shared his distaste. This seemed the perfect way to drive a wedge between yachties and a large slice of the local community.

We visited yet another local museum. Surprisingly for such a swanky town this was an interestingly scruffy affair, open one afternoon a week, with an odd rag-bag collection of artefacts all jumbled up together. The most interesting part of our visit was our conversation with the curator, which highlighted the differences in thinking between the British and the Irish and the historical reasons for this.

Liz Windsor had just visited Ireland. As usual I paid this about as much attention as any celeb news in the gossip columns. After all she's always jetting off on jollies to various parts of the world. As a republican this was a really big deal to the curator, who thought that such a thing could never have happened in his lifetime. He was extremely positive about it, suggesting that it represented a rapprochement between the countries and was a highly significant historical event. I don't think many people in Britain would consider such a rapprochement even necessary. In this the Scots join the English in the sort of blindness to oppression that the English have in their relationship with Scotland. (Read the last sentence again if you're not sure. You don't have to agree with it, but It does make grammatical sense, I think.)

The Spaniard pub, Scilly, Kinsale. There's still a lot of references to the nation that helped fight the English

Kinsale

Aside from an odd collection of hand tools, the museum's major exhibit was on the sinking of the Lusitania eleven miles off the Old Head of Kinsale by a German 'U' boat in 1915. The exhibit included a closely argued analysis of the justification for the sinking. It concluded that there was blame on both sides and that the 'U' boat captain had reason to believe that the ostensibly civilian passage concealed some military aims. Again it is unthinkable that such an analysis would be presented in a British museum, where it would be quite clear - British good, Jerries bad - without the need actually to think about it. We often need to be reminded that Ireland is a properly foreign country.

Kinsale is also filled with Spanish references in the names of pubs and streets. In 1601 the siege of Kinsale involved Irish and Spanish troops defending the city for three months against the English army. Their defeat more-or-less represented the final conquest of Ireland by England, which perhaps makes the high profile of the event in the tourist literature surprising. But you're probably still likely to get a better reception in the town if you're Spanish than if you're English.

The next day Fiona got the bus to the airport, which left from about fifty yards from the marina, at the end of her week, in which we'd done 224 miles in six passages. I spent the following day, my birthday, in the exotic pursuit of trying to clean some of the crap off Zoph which she'd accumulated since leaving Port Ed.

Fort George remains a monument to the battle that ended Irish independence

I chatted to the crews on a couple of the racy boats which had apparently gathered for the season's main regatta the previous weekend. Kinsale and Cork have big events on alternate years. A couple of stragglers were still waiting for the weather to head back to the Bristol Channel or the south coast of England.

I received an unexpected email from a bloke I've never met saying "Happy 54th birthday Martin". This was from a couple cruising the coast of Norway as far north as Lofoten, Sweden, Denmark, Germany and the Netherlands who were, apparently, using the rants I had written about my previous trips as a sort of pilot book of Scandinavia. In one of these rants I had obviously mentioned my 50th birthday and he had picked this up. Jolly nice of him if a tad foolish using my scribblings as a navigation aid. I hoped that I wouldn't lead him onto the rocks anywhere.

The following day Anna flew in for a long weekend. By plane you understand. After another pleasant night in Kinsale I gritted my teeth to pay the considerable bill for three nights in the marina. We motorsailed gently out of Kinsale for the short trip to Crosshaven on the oddly named Owenboy River in Cork Harbour. It was a lovely hot sunny day, but there was barely enough wind to sail, so the engine stayed on for most of the eighteen mile passage. We passed into the more sheltered waters behind the Old Head of Kinsale (nobody could tell me, incidentally, where the New Head of Kinsale is) and into Cork Harbour. There's three marinas in the very sheltered inlet, which is at the epicentre of Ireland's sailing and as busy as a bit of the Solent. We plumped for the marina with ostensibly the best facilities at the Royal Cork Yacht Club.

The RCYC is the oldest yacht club in the world and judging by the inside leg measurements of their members I can confirm that this is indeed the case. Founded in 1720 it's members have the distinction of having, on average, the shortest legs of any yacht club in the world. My evidence for this is the sheer number of boarding steps on the pontoons. Some of the boats are quite big but it's not billionaire's row and there's quite a lot of lowish freeboard, racy boats designed for nipping round the cans in the bay. Yet about 50% of them apparently need boarding steps fixed to the pontoons. These sturdy constructions of between two and five steps are often personalised with the yacht's name. I can think of no other explanation for this phenomenon than that the club members' legs have been worn down short during their truly prodigious lifetimes.

The club house is rather swanky and is apparently the place to be seen for Sunday lunch, but enquiries suggested no opportunities for mere visitors to eat here and we were directed firmly to the world's slowest chippy in the local run down seaside town of Crosshaven. The club's facilities were good however, though there were signs of considerable eccentricity amongst the members. Chief amongst these was a sign on the toilet door which read "Strictly Adults Only - Baby Changing Area". I never established whether an adults only baby changing facility was needed for the oldest and most incontinent members who had first joined in 1720, or if the club was frequented by British peers of the realm and Tory MPs who had taken to dressing up as babies as a lifestyle choice.

Though the wee town itself has seen better days there's an abundance of posh suburban houses lining the sides of the inlet at Crosshaven and a walk to the headland reveals the huge quantities of money which have flooded into the country until recently. There's plenty of brand new modern domestic follies designed by architects whose brief didn't include keeping the costs down.

The next day we pootled slowly under motor up the Owenboy River to Drake's Pool where, apparently, Francis Drake had hidden a whole fleet in the shallows amongst the trees from the Spanish fleet. Given the history and the fact that the English were undoubtedly the baddies it's quite surprising that it retains his name. As we headed further and further up river into the shallows the boats got reassuringly smaller and scruffier. Drake's pool is billed as a major beauty spot. It is however somewhat marred by the main road running all round it, which isn't mentioned in the pilot.

We headed back past the marinas. It was a beautiful, warm, sunny Sunday in July, around mid day and perhaps one or two percent of the yachts were out sailing. It was later confirmed by a local that scarcely any boats ever leave their pontoons. Apparently there's hardly even any racing nowadays. This was put down to the economy, which I found puzzling. If you own a boat you still have to pay for it whether you use it or not. The marginal costs of going out for a sail are virtually nil and you might as well go out for a spin to help you forget for an hour or two that your financial services company is rapidly going to the wall.

We continued across to the east end of Cork Harbour and the less imaginatively named East Channel. As a sheltered piece of inland water I had thought that Cork Harbour would be a mass of boats. In fact it's quite shallow and crossed by various shipping channels, so most of the sailing actually happens outside the harbour in the bit of sea sheltered behind Kinsale Head. We passed East Ferry (which joins the illustrious company of Strome, Queen's and Otter in that it doesn't actually have a ferry) and stemmed the ebb tide up to the wide shallow pool to the north, in which there are several anchorages. On a mooring I spotted the Vancouver *"Islander"*, which is I believe the first Vancouver 28 ever built. In my enthusiasm to get closer and take a squint at her I succeeded in running aground. On soft sand but on a falling tide. A few minutes frantic razzing of the engine freed us and I hoped - probably futilely - that the spot was sufficiently remote for no-one to have noticed.

Dubious practices amongst the world's oldest yachties

We took the tide back down to the slightly scruffy but attractive East Ferry marina for the night. A bloke off a suitably scruffy local motor-sailer 'helped' with the lines. This involved holding the bow so tightly against the pontoon that he gouged a chunk out of the gelcoat on one of the handily placed rusty nails. This facility has been built on the river by a friendly farmer who has spotted that there's more money to be made from yachties than from cows and manages the whole fifty berth marina himself. It was mostly filled with local boats which restrict themselves to pottering around Cork Harbour, but we were invited aboard one beautiful home built 45ft yacht based, according to its skipper, on an Oyster design.

Said skipper was a very charming, friendly, soft spoken chap pushing sixty with beige clothes, beige hair, beige skin and a beige voice who it is impossible to believe was not an Irish daytime telly presenter. He had built the boat from scratch in his garden near Dublin and was now embarking on a trip round Ireland the opposite way to us. This was not without its dangers. Within five minutes of inviting us on board, as Anna desperately tried to avoid spilling his rather expensive red wine on a white leather cockpit settee, an idiot numpty with little idea how to steer his tiny yacht had been swept down by the tide and rammed the Oyster's stern. One of the penalties of having a large yacht is the need to moor to the outside of main pontoons, where you are more vulnerable. The skipper remained unflappable.

East Ferry

Aside from a pleasant rural environment there was little to keep us in East Ferry so the following day we headed across Cork Harbour and up the river Lee to the centre of Cork, where there is a big new pontoon operated by the Council. We were there on the recommendation of the Men in Black who had boarded Zoph a few days before. On the way we passed the city of Cobh which, when I first saw it on a map, I assumed was an Irish spelling of Cork but is in fact a separate city.

We passed hundreds of sprogs sailing toppers and lasers in the strong tides of the River Lee. With usual bad timing we followed the channel across the drying shallows for what seemed like miles against the two knot tide. We skirted the industrial docks on the outskirts of town. We passed fishermen in old rowing boats waterproofed with tarred canvas fishing with small nets stretched from the shore of the river. One of them held up a large salmon to show us as we passed. We passed more industrial docks where ships were being noisily loaded right in the heart of the city. Eventually we arrived at the end of the line, the large new pontoon just before the first low bridge that blocked the river. Sandwiched between a main road and a loading dock the pontoon had one occupant, the grey customs ship which had boarded us. Needless to say it contributed to the din by running its engines all night instead of plugging into the readily available mains electricity. I should have been more wary about tourist advice provided by the border patrol.

Since I had pictured the upper reaches of the river in the centre of town as being lined with trendy pubs and restaurants, the industrial landscape was a little disappointing, but the pontoon is pretty much in the middle of town, the attractions of which are but a short walk away. Having said that, the attractions of Cork were themselves not much worth writing home about. It's a pleasant enough city to wander in, but not a lovely one. It perhaps suffers from the lack of a really old built fabric - the legacy of having been a colony for so long.

One boat, a wee French Beneteau, joined us on the pontoon the next morning. -Anna jumped ship in Cork and caught a bus to the airport while I headed back down river, again, of course, against a two knot tide. The wind was mostly on the beam but varying from five to twenty four knots and in the absolutely pissing down rain. Stair rods flattened the surface of the water as they bounced off it. Another yacht passed sailing up river with the tide.

Fishermen in the suburbs of Cork

Cobh

We sailed past the naval dockyards near Cobh. As we passed one sinister grey shooty-ship with its gun turrets pointing skywards I noticed something odd about its crew. High up on the deck of this massive military vessel was one, single, unaccompanied person. A one year old toddler was running backwards and forwards along the deck, toppling over occasionally and hauling himself to his feet for another totter. Try as I might I couldn't see any other occupants of the ship. Presumably he'd been left on watch while the rest of the crew went down the pub.

The RCYC pontoon was marred only by the presence of increasing numbers of large American yachts crewed by stereotypically loud, brash Americans. The idiot crewmember of one large yacht from Occupied Northern Mexico tried to help by taking my lines but clearly had no idea what to do with them. Annoyingly, the skipper of this yacht instantly recognised Zoph as a Vancouver 27 and said repeatedly what great boats they were, which made it irritatingly difficult to be offhand with him.

A Gigantic Whinge on the Celtic Fringe 71

The grounds of Cork University

Cork

Irish Sat-Nav

Sorry. I know Irish jokes are beneath me but I saw this car in Crosshaven and...

(Occupied Northern Mexico, by the way, is nowadays more usually known as California. The Americans nicked it and some other bits from Mexico in 1848, mostly to help them run their lucrative slave trade. It's a long shot but I'm trying to resurrect this issue as an international dispute).

Round Ireland's Arse

I was stuck in Crosshaven for three nights. The first day was what I believe is nowadays known as a knob-rainer. The forecast was for southerly gales and I had to make quite a long passage along an exposed lee shore. There's not that many secure places for a yacht eastwards along the coast. Waterford, which had just hosted the tall ships race, is ten miles up river from the sea. Youghal is said to be exposed to swell and other fishing harbours don't seem to be much recommended. This left Kilmore Quay, some seventy miles away, as my next destination. Flying solo you want quite benign conditions for such a long trip, which necessitates a decent average speed.

The second day the forecast was for force five to seven from the south west. Feeling a bit of a wimp I decided to stay in Crosshaven's perfect shelter again, despite the fact that the wind would have been more or less behind me. It was an annoying sort of day on which gentle zephyrs barely managed to cross the treed peninsula to the south to rustle the leaves on shore and I had little sense of anything bigger out to sea, but I stayed put nonetheless.

The best forecast you can get when you are cruising from a secure anchorage is a force three or four from somewhere behind you. The second best forecast is a force eleven right on the nose. Then there's no problem making a decision. It's simple. You just stay put. But forecasts are never like this. They're always force four behind you backing force five on the nose, perhaps force six later. Or force five on the beam backing on to the nose and increasing 'at times'. As often as not what time they will increase is unspecified. Crucially, there's always much worse coming the following day or the day after, forcing you to go in poorer conditions than you'd wish.

But I sat put for a day in the still air. On the positive side I did get my bike fixed for nothing with the help of a huge fat bloke in a wee bike shop in Crosshaven. Even in these more urban and urbane parts the Irish seem friendly to foreigners and he refused to accept any money for supplying parts and advice.

On the third day I left Crosshaven at five a.m. to take the last of the ebb out of Cork Harbour. With the wind at twelve to twenty knots true from the west I still needed to motorsail most of the day to keep up a decent average speed. It was a day of dodging showers and squalls and for quite a while we were successful Eventually and

Roche's Point

inevitably however, one dumped itself on us, complete with its fickle winds going from five to twenty five knots in seconds. Otherwise it was a reasonably uneventful passage, with one other yacht appearing out of Waterford and also heading east.

As I got closer to Kilmore Quay, a fishing port with a small marina just near Ireland's coccyx and sticking out on what looks like an exposed point of land, I got a bit concerned about the final approach. The south westerly swell left over from the gale was still a couple of metres high and the approach from the south skirts a lot of rocks off a shallow lee shore. I needn't have worried. As I passed through the rocks on the approach the sea magically fell quiet. It was like when we had rounded the corner onto the south coast and again when we passed round Old Head of Kinsale. With each milestone the sea was beginning to behave itself more and more and be more like what most of us are used to in the sheltered waters of Scotland.

Kilmore Quay is a perfectly good marina and a good place to wait for weather. The village also has its twee bits, with thatched cottages. But the village and harbour have a bit of a run-down feel. Here you do get the sense of an economy in decline. Two of the three pubs were shut and boarded up and the third, a newish two star hotel with pretensions, such a hellhole of live country and western and karaoke as to be virtually uninhabitable. Other attractions included the annual 'FishFest', due to start the next morning and for which several blokes in battered old transit vans were erecting stalls. I think it was real and not a plot line from Father Ted. Such a shame that I would miss this heady excitement. A hugely overblown memorial garden, listing the names of just about everyone lost at sea off the coast of the whole of Ireland in the last two centuries, was just tacky enough to feel sad in the wrong sort of way.

Oddly, there were dozens of camper vans gathered. Mostly these were rather scruffy affairs and there was little evidence of foreign tourism, but for some reason Kilmore Quay attracts large numbers of itinerant tourists. Back at the harbour, the large numbers of fishing boats ran their engines all night for no apparent reason, detracting from any sympathy you might have for their falling catches and hard times. The marina manny demanded €30 a night for my eight metre boat. Practically an all time record and unjustified by the quality of the place.

On the pontoon another boat arrived, a Hallberg Rassy down from Dublin. We got talking and I was invited aboard for a beer. It transpired that they had cruised the west of Scotland extensively and had befriended one yacht from Port Edgar, the wee green-fringed racer *'Kermit'*. They had, it seemed spent some time getting drunk one midsummer's night with George Fyfe, Cap'n Kermit, at anchor in Loch Drumbuie, near Tobermory.

I remembered one encounter with Cap'n Kermit back at Port Edgar. Sitting aboard Zoph I had heard the low, undulating moan of a seal. There's a lot of seals on the Forth and you quite often hear them moaning on rocks, but this one seemed to be in the marina and in obvious distress. It kept on letting out long groans of apparent pain, starting low, rising to a plaintive, haunting howl and dying away to a despairing wail. This cycle was repeated endlessly. I wandered the pontoons looking for signs of the obviously teminally injured creature but it wasn't easy to find. The eerie racket filled the air and seemed to be coming from all directions at once. Eventually I found the source of the nightmarish howling. George was sitting aboard Kermit 'singing'. What he was singing was anybody's guess, but apparently the distressing banshee groans were intended as music. It is to be hoped that the air was not rent by this racket that midsummer's night in Loch Drumbuie

Is this butcher genuinely called Mr. Kidney? I really hope so

Parts of Kilmore Quay were twee

The reason for going round Ireland anti-clockwise, against the advice of some, had been to give myself options. When I reached Ireland's south east corner, I thought, I could take the easy option and head up the Irish Sea. I could head for the wild unknown of the English south coast and back up the crappy east coast of England to the Forth, or I could keep going south. I had the charts for it. A chip for the chart plotter and second hand paper charts which would see me all the way to the Canaries. At the back of my mind this was always the aim. To continue to France, Spain, Portugal and on southwards.

On reflection however, I found that I was getting a bit worn down by long solo passages in biggish swells. A couple of thousand miles along the coast of Norway is no big deal. From nearly everywhere on that coast you can leave more or less whatever the weather and whatever time you like, without worrying about tides or swell. You can travel for as long as you want and stop whenever you want. The west of Ireland hadn't been like that and neither would the Atlantic coasts of France and Iberia. On reflection I decided that, even if the boat was prepared for such a trip, psychologically I wasn't. For this year I'd take the easy option and head back up the Irish Sea. Kilmore Quay was the turning point. The last point at which I could sensibly make that decision.

So it was with some sense of regret that I left Kilmore Quay the next morning motorsailing under full sail. Several other boats had been waiting there for the weather and were also leaving that morning, but typically they were all going in different directions. One boat was making straight for Brittany. An

English and an American yacht were both heading for the Scilly Isles. A bloke sailing solo on an Etap 21 was heading across to Fishguard in south Wales and I was heading north for Arklow. Between us we were making for practically every bit of the Gaelic fringe, including the Garlic fringe. As I headed across the shallow channel of St Patrick's Bridge, inshore of the Saltee Islands, the lonely Etap headed out to sea under spinnaker, a long solo trip for such a wee boat.

Once again the sea state changed as I reached a milestone. After Carnsore point, on the very south-eastern tip of Ireland, the sea fell away further to what seemed like a mill pond after the swell of the south coast. We were finally in the Irish Sea. There was less tide against us than I expected, then up to 2.5 knots with us as we headed north. This was handy, as with a fifty two mile passage I wanted to keep up a decent average speed. The forecast was for north west winds of force three to four. Of course northerlies would have been absolutely perfect for the last month as I headed southwards. I didn't get any in the forecast, however, until the very day I turned north. To be fair however in the event we had bugger-all wind for most of the day, but for the last hour or so it suddenly filled from the south south east and rose to a solid force five. This was pretty handy for us and we sped along on a broad reach. A pain in the arse for anyone heading south and expecting a north westerly, but who cares about them?

It was a Saturday afternoon and a few boats were sailing out of Arklow. We entered the river and tied to the long pontoon just outside the very tight, small, newish marina. There were several cruising boats on the pontoon including a big scruffy uncommunicative thing from Shetland and a solo German in a Bavaria so old it was only seven metres long. I didn't know they made them so small. In an example to us all he said he was sailing 'around England'. Since he went through the Forth-Clyde he was, strictly speaking, sailing round England, Wales and a bit of Scotland. The crucial thing is however that he didn't claim to be sailing round the UK.

Arklow is, to be frank, a dump. It was the only town I saw in Ireland that merited the title. The town centre had a run-down feel that, for once, didn't attract me into its pubs. It really felt like a small industrial town on the way down. It felt... oh I don't know... like... like half the small towns in Britain.

Never one to go for the easy option I'd decided to head across to North Wales. The easy route up the Irish Sea is on the Irish side, on a deep, weather shore with harbours and marinas. Cardigan bay is, by contrast, a shallow, drying, exposed lee shore. My Mother, however, was born and brought up in Porthmadog, at the root of the Llŷn peninsula and since I was a child I'd always fancied the idea of sailing into its pictureskew but drying harbour. The fact that you can make such decisions is one of the great things about cruising. Without the need for tickets or prior organisation, as long as you've got the charts and the forecast, you can decide on a whim to head for another country.

Rounding Carnsore Point to head north

It also highlighted the closeness of the elements of the Celtic Fringe to one another. Wales was just a day away across the Irish sea. Another consideration was the extreme cost of berthing in the marinas around Dublin, further to the north. So I determined to leave Ireland at Arklow and continue my complete circumnavigation of the UK and Ireland by the slightly truncated Irish route, on the east side of the Irish Sea.

Another of the cruising boats in Arklow was over from Abersoch on the Llŷn Peninsula - or "Abersock on the Lin Peninsula", as they called it - and I quizzed them on making landfall there. Of course they were English, not Welsh. In common with all the touros in North Wales they were from one of the industrial cities in the north west or midlands of England. They explained to me that the Welsh were mostly sheep-shaggers who only spoke Welsh when English people were within hearing just to annoy them, but that there was a big marina at Pwllheli - or "Poo-Helly", as they pronounced it. It's about fifty miles in a straight line from Arklow to Wales, about another twenty five to Pwllheli. Talking to them I realised that I was crossing the Irish Sea to the front line of the Celtic Fringe, where it clashed most violently with the Anglic bits to the east.

The Front line of the Celtic Fringe

I left Arklow at the unholy hour of five a.m. as the day dawned into that rarest of things in 2011, a proper summer's day. All day the sun shone out of a clear sky and I motored with the main up and no wind at all towards the shallow Arklow Bank. The east coast of Ireland is fringed by an annoying sweep of sandbanks about five or six miles off the coast, of which the Arklow Bank is one. Here the sea shallows to about three metres on the chart, but the shifting sands can make it shallower. There's potentially big overfalls over the bank with the strong tides and a long row of huge new wind turbines has been built atop it. The recommended route is to make a long detour and pass either north or south of it. With seventy five miles to run and in perfect conditions I just went right across the middle between a couple of the turbines, slowing down to watch the echo sounder record one metre under the keel as we passed in the shadow of a wind turbine.

The tide runs surprisingly strongly up and down the Irish Sea. With twelve metre tides in the Bristol Channel, the Mersey and Morecambe bay, an awful lot of water has to swill around over a six hour tide, so in the middle between Ireland and the Llŷn Peninsula it flows at up to 3.5 knots. Since this was a two tide trip there was little point in fighting it, so the most efficient path was to let the tide take me north and then south, arriving well to the south of Pwllheli to avoid having to fight the ebb sweeping west along the peninsula. So I set a compass course and just ignored the fact that the track over the bottom was way off line, banking on the tide to put me back on course eventually. For once my strategy was spot on and Zoph described a perfect sine curve on the chart plotter as she swept first north, then south, then north again towards Pwllheli. The course over the ground changed by around thirty degrees without my touching the trusty tillerpilot at all.

I saw three or four yachts heading in various directions and three or four ships appeared on the AIS heading up or down the Irish Sea. I didn't see a single fishing boat all day, which was unusual. Indeed in the whole of my stay in Wales I saw very few fishing boats. Whether it's the lack of fish or the lack of good all weather ports in Cardigan Bay to fish from I'm not sure.

We swept south of Bardsey Island then northwards at a good pace. As we passed Abersoch the scene was one of a good old fashioned seaside summer day. It was Sunday and the wide sweep of pure white sand along the coast was dotted with lobster-coloured people. The sea was littered with a huge variety of mostly unseaworthy craft, from lilos to sailing dinghies to execrable jet skis to speedboats. Out of the middle of this throng, in the light zephyr airs, sailed a fleet of forty three elegant, streamlined Dragons. It was the most activity I'd seen on the water all year and a fantastic welcome to Wales. I discovered later that the Dragons - and I know there were forty three of them because I looked it up later - were from Japan, Australia, Russia, Ireland and the UK and were engaged, coincidentally, in competing for the Edinburgh Cup. They certainly made a pleasant backdrop for one Edinburgh boat's arrival as we motored up the shallow, silted channel to Pwllheli Marina on a falling tide, just in time to make sure we had enough water.

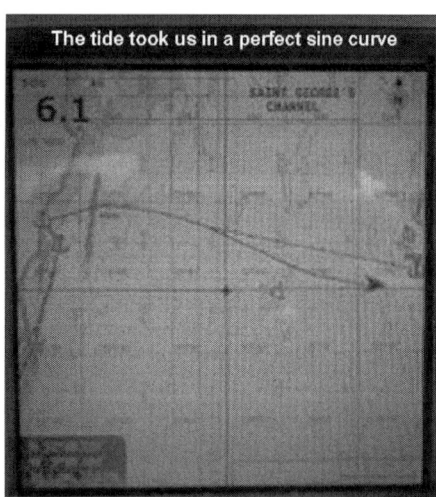

Gingerly crossing the Arklow Bank 6 miles off shore

The tide took us in a perfect sine curve

It had taken three days from Crosshaven to Pwllheli, during which Zoph had been a total of 195.8 miles. Easily a record for my solo passages, none of which have been overnight.

If North Wales is on the front line of the Celtic Fringe, Pwllheli is occupied territory. The town, a mile from the white sandy beaches across an abandoned, mud-silted old dock, has always been fairly unprepossessing. Now it largely consists of a bus station surrounded by an old Edwardian shopping arcade that has been shut down and abandoned, boarded up pound shops and a selection of dire pubs and rough chippies. In summer the local population is nowhere to be seen, replaced by the mass youth of Brum, Manchester and Liverpool. They spill out from the camp sites, endless ranks of caravans and low rent boarding houses. Unlovely and unloved, Pwllheli looks like it's well on its way downhill.

A mile away across the deserted, mud-silted docks sits Pwllheli marina, the single largest, brashest, most expensive collection of bad taste over-powered motorised gin palaces and boy-racer floating noise machines that I have ever seen outside the Mediterranean. There's quite a number of sailing boats as well, but no marina in Britain can have such a high proportion of power boats. They aren't scruffy ones either. From the multi-million pound three storey gleaming floating mansion to the two seater open speedboat with go faster stripes, each represents conspicuous consumption and a loads-a-money culture. It's the most surreal collection of floating nonsense in this unremarkable backwater, with its silting channel and shallow coast exposed to south westerlies.

I'm not really clear where all this money comes from. Undoubtedly the people are from the industrial midlands and north west of England. Indeed many of them were in evidence lounging on deck disporting their beer bellies or noisily towing their shrieking offspring behind speedboats in huge inflatable doughnuts. My theory, neither confirmed nor denied by those I spoke to, was that most of the 'boats' belong to footballers and ex-footballers - overpaid but not in the most obscenely wealthy bracket - who hanker after a billionaire gin palace in the Med but can only afford a million pound speedboat in Pwllheli.

After the sheer amount of money parked in the marina, the second thing that strikes you is the total lack of connection between the marina and the town. The tumbleweed blows slowly down the deserted, potholed streets between the two, along the old deserted dock. Why would this crowd of brash, bad taste sun-seekers bother with the town? The marina has a sailing club with a bar and restaurant, a chandler, various other businesses and facilities. These include a big bog block into which Radio Two is piped twenty four hours a day. Having a crap to the cheery sound of Ken Bruce ministering to the dottled and decrepit on Radio Tomb was quite a surreal experience. The denizens of the marina drive their BMWs from their homes to their boats without their feet touching the ground. They play in the sea and on the beaches and then drive straight home. Their effect on the local economy - apart from providing employment in the marina - is zero.

Perhaps surprisingly, this seems to be how the local people - and local businesses - like it. Various people told me that the original plan had been to put the marina in the old dock near the centre of town. This would have involved a lot of dredging and given the town a huge aesthetic and economic boost. But local businesses objected. They didn't want a load of Brum beach bums clogging up their town. The consensus was that they seemed to prefer to continue in gentle stagnation. Instead the marina was located a mile from town and the old docks were left to rot. Now the Council are refusing to carry out any more dredging, the marina has gone from all tides access to half tide access and there's a danger of it silting up altogether.

A couple of people I spoke to on boats were incredulous as to why this should be, yet it seemed to me that their very protestations provided the answer. "The bloody sheep-shaggers seem to resent us for some reason, yet they need our money. Their economy relies on tourism and we have a load more money than them, so I don't understand why they resent us so much". I tried to explain to them that jumping up and down waving huge wads of money in the air and shouting "Like me, you sheep-shagging bastards, I'm richer than you" is not considered the most sure fire way of making friends.

Many people in different parts of the Celtic Fringe may feel that their culture is under threat from incomers, but in North Wales it really is. It takes quite an effort for urbanites - be they from England, the Central Belt or abroad - to reach the ostensibly Gaelic speaking bits of Scotland. When they do get there most of them are quite interested in the culture. They may patronise it a bit and treat it simplistically and stereotypically, but they aren't overtly fighting against it. Most of the touros from abroad who reach the west of Ireland are specifically in it for the culture. Again they may demand that the locals prance about like leprechauns for their amusement, but they are genuinely interested in the music and the history.

North Wales is different. This is mass tourism. The Llŷn Peninsula has white sand beaches and cheap caravan sites. When I was a lad it was a half-day trip from the border with England, now it's three quarters of an hour from the English border to the border of the westernmost county, Gwynedd. It's an hour and a half and two hours respectively from the suburbs of Liverpool and Manchester to the Llŷn Peninsula. From some of England's biggest cities to the very heart of the Welsh speaking bit of Wales is practically a commute. And the tourists don't come here because of their deep interest in Welsh culture, history and music. They come to the coast for the sea and the beaches. The Celts are a mere annoyance and a laughable one at that. To your average English bigot the Scots may be mean drunks, but they are also Cabinet Ministers and captains of industry and therefore a threat. The Welsh, on the other hand, even in their own land, are seen as just a bit of a joke.

So the local people stay out of the way and wish longingly for the end of the school holidays and the winter so that they can once more take possession of their communities and walk the streets with impunity. Astonishingly, given this pressure, there's more native Celtic spoken in this corner of Wales than in all the other bits of the Celtic Fringe put together, but more of that later, in Porthmadog, epicentre of the Welsh speaking world.

Ancestral Home

The next day, for once, the acres of overpriced motorised plastic in the marina didn't look too out of place, as the sun beat down from a cloudless sky on a Mediterranean scene. I left under full sail once the tide had risen enough and set sail for Porthmadog. Snowdon rises to 3560 feet some nine miles behind Porthmadog, whilst the coast is fringed with a line of pure white sand wherever you look. I've only ever approached Porthmadog from the land before and it's not that impressive. There's a wide strip of low lying, somewhat boggy land between the coast and the mountains, on part of which my Grandfather ('Taid' in Welsh) had his small sheep farm. But from the sea on a day like that one in July it's spectacular. The clear air foreshortened the view and Snowdon rose steeply behind white painted cottages, blindingly white sand and an azure blue sea.

The Welsh slate which roofed half the world used to leave Porthmadog in sailing ships, which is pretty astonishing given its general crapness as a commercial port. Though a beautiful inlet, the Glaslyn Estuary is completely drying and can be entered for only an hour or two around high tide, along a snaking, twisting channel which appeared, at high tide, to begin way out at sea. Every year the sandbanks shift and the channel markers are moved. Exposed to the south west the bar is presumably a nightmare in even quite moderate conditions, but as I sailed towards it under full sail in about eight knots of breeze from the north there was scarcely a ripple.

In such a channel a chart plotter is something of a disadvantage. As you follow the frequent port and starboard channel markers a glimpse at the chart shows that you are miles off the charted channel and crossing drying banks that are virtually land. Though the channel markers are moved annually, the charted depths are changed once a century or so.

Snowdon behind white sand beaches

Approaching Porthmadog

Porthmadog is a very attractive slate-built harbour that's mostly drying, with some deeper patches. Though the approach is packed with speedboats for sale, these are mostly destined for Pwllheli and Abersoch and the moorings in the harbour secure a reasonably motley collection of mostly ageing, scruffy, smallish boats. My older relatives, brought up here in the 1930s, are filled with dire tales of the seedy working harbour, a no-go area for sprogs with its dodgy characters and red lights. Now it's a no-go area because it's as twee as can be and rammed with touros.

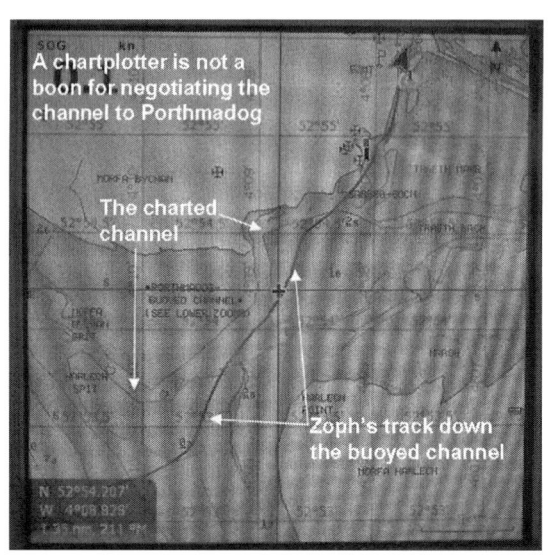

A chartplotter is not a boon for negotiating the channel to Porthmadog

The charted channel

Zoph's track down the buoyed channel

I had phoned first the harbourmaster, then the sailing club at Porthmadog and the latter had offered the choice of either a mooring, on which Zoph could remain afloat at low water neaps, or a pontoon berth with about three feet of water for Zoph's four foot six inch draught. I chose the latter as I had invited elderly rellies aboard for tea. On my approach to the harbour the phone rang: my uncle had had a turn. The medic had been called and he was better now, but in no state for anything nautical.

I said that instead I'd visit my rellies for tea, in the ancestral home where my mother was raised and where I remember spending summer weeks from the age of five. I decided to cycle and allowed half an hour. Five minutes later I arrived. The geography of Porthmadog has shrunk over the years. When I was five it was miles and miles to the end of the farm lane and the harbour was practically the other side of the country. Now the track is a couple of hundred yards long and the harbour half a mile away. Something to do with continental drift I imagine.

From the outside virtually nothing about the small, grey farmhouse on the flat land at the base of the Snowdonia hills has changed for at least half a century. I walked between the same rough slate gateposts and across the same huge slate flags as I did fifty years ago and had seen on photographs of the 1930s. Inside lots has changed. I'm really showing my age here, but I genuinely remember when bath night was once a week on a Saturday. The old zinc tub was taken from its hook on the wall in the kitchen, filled with water heated on the stove and us kids took it in turns to have a bath. It paid to be amongst the oldest. The youngest wallowed in the foetid stench of the soap and filth emulsion washed off the older ones.

Waiting to dry out in Porthmadog

Ancestral home

The cludgie was a chemical one accessed in the most awkward possible way. You had to leave by the front door, wade across the cow-shit filled farmyard, squeeze through an old gate into the back garden then push your way through the three foot high nettles for about fifty yards to a shed full of holes, a bucket of poo and bits of newspaper hung on a nail in the wall.

It was fantastic. I used to love staying there despite the bog. Admittedly I was only there in the summer and, at the age of seven, I didn't drink enough beer to warrant getting up for a widdle in the middle of the night, but it was such a different world. There were haystacks to make dens in, trees to climb and, by the age of eleven, hidden corners in the woods to light fires, burn tatties and sausages and share packets of ten Carlton Premium fags in.

Now the land is part of the bigger farm up the road and the back garden is clipped lawns and flower beds, but it still brought back memories.

Though practically within modern commuting distance of the industrial cities of England, Porthmadog remains at the very epicentre of the Celtic world. I'm willing to bet that a higher proportion of the indigenous population speaks a Celtic language than anywhere else in Wales, Ireland, Scotland, Cornwall or the Garlic Fringe. The Council is very PC about it and promotes the speaking of Welsh in schools and elsewhere, but to the denizens of Porthmadog English remains very definitely a second language. For the first eleven years or so of their lives most are monoglot Welsh speakers.

Here's couple of examples to stress the point. From the age of about seven I would spend a week each year with my relatives in Porthmadog by myself, my parents doubtless relieved to divest themselves of an annoying brat for a short time. I got on fine with my cousins, a couple of whom were about the same age as me. We played in the haystack, climbed trees and later learned the arts of arson and smoking. Being a useless monoglot I never learned any Welsh at all. And none of them spoke a word of English. Year after year we would get on fine in each other's company without either party understanding a word spoken by the other. To them English was very definitely a completely foreign language. They only started to learn it, as most people in Britain learn French, at secondary school.

Porthmadog Harbour

Old fashioned seaside complete with beach huts

To this day my relatives need to concentrate quite hard to speak English and can't quite manage it if under any sort of stress. This point was made particularly starkly a few years ago when my uncle, my Mother's brother, had a stroke. Uncle Griff emigrated to Canada in the early 1950s. He took up farming there in, naturally, an English speaking community. He produced a pile of English speaking sprogs and grand-sprogs and spent the next forty five years or so speaking nothing but English. Then he had a stroke. After it and for the rest of his life he never spoke another word of English. He could only speak Welsh. The words of the second language had entirely disappeared from some superficial part of his memory whilst the deeply embedded vocabulary of his first language, learned from birth, remained intact.

More than anywhere else on the Celtic Fringe the two worlds - of indigenous inhabitants and incomers - remain as separate cultures. Different groups with different languages, aspirations and purposes. One carrying on with life virtually in the shadows, waiting for the winter when they have a better chance of re-inhabiting their invaded land, the other complaining that the bloody sheep-shaggers only talk Welsh in the shops to annoy them.

I cycled back to Zoph from this place so redolent with memories and sat aboard waiting for her to dry out on the pontoon and hoping I'd got the lines secured right. I hoped that she'd touch the bottom and remain upright alongside on the sandy floor of the harbour. With three feet of water she should retain enough buoyancy not to fall over. Low water was just after midnight so I waited and watched the depth on the echo sounder. You must bear in mind when considering what follows that I'm a very stupid person. I watched the water depth go down from two metres to 1.8 to 1.6 to 1.4. Here it stayed for quite a while and I concluded that the tide must have fallen as far as it was going to and by lucky chance the water remained 1.4 metres deep, which is just about exactly Zoph's draught.

Smugly pleased with my calculations I stepped in the dark over the side onto the pontoon which, the discerning amongst you will have realised, wasn't there. Zoph was sitting bolt upright on the sand, but the pontoon had disappeared downwards about eighteen inches. Blindingly obviously to anyone with a brain, once the boat is firmly on the bottom, the echo sounder will not continue to record the falling water depth.

Not wanting to leave on the morning high tide at six a.m. I spent most of the next day exploring Porthmadog and its environs. In common with various place on the Atlantic fringe of Europe, Porthmadog lays claim to be the departure point for the 'discovery' of the Americas by Europeans. How you can claim to have 'discovered' a continent if it's already full of people when you get there is a moot point. Madog ab Owain Gwynedd is supposed to have sailed there in about 1170, afterwards lending his name to the town of Porthmadog. Unfortunately Porthmadog - or Portmadoc as it is spelled in English, was founded in the nineteenth century as a port for the slate trade by an English bloke called William Madocks. Draw your own conclusions.

Of course it's well known that various Vikings laid claim to the discovery of the continent. In Fenit, on the west of Ireland, I had stood next to a statue of St Brendan the Mad Drug-Addled Navigator, who is supposed to have sailed from there to the Americas in about 520a.d, searching for the Garden of Eden and tussling with mythical sea monsters. What puzzles me is why so many people are prepared to admit to 'discovering' America. Have they no shame at all? There can be little doubt that it would have been better for all concerned, especially the people who originally lived there, if it had remained undiscovered.

I headed out on the end of the flood at five p.m. The impracticality of sailing in these beautiful surroundings was demonstrated by another wee yacht that left the harbour at speed as soon as there was enough water. They were heading twenty miles away to Barmouth for the night. To do so they had to cross St Patrick's Causeway, a long line of mostly drying sandbanks which stretches fully twenty miles out from the coast and whose name emphasises the connection with Ireland. They then had to be in Barmouth before the tide fell too far. It will not come as a surprise that there is a bar at Barmouth, then a tortuous buoyed channel over drying banks. If they didn't make enough speed to cross the bar on time there was nowhere else to go within fifty miles until the next high tide in the morning. As they shot off southwards I had a very pleasant evening reach at four knots back to Pwllheli for the night.

It was still summer - for the third day in a row - and the night was filled with the sound of drunken teenagers in swimming gear sitting around in huge inflatable doughnuts designed to be towed behind speedboats, whilst Daddy's gin palace, all its glass patio doors slid open, belched loud music out into the night. Eventually, after midnight, I turned into a grumpy old sod and went and told them to shut up. To my surprise and, perversely, annoyance, they did so immediately. Oh shit, I've turned into an elderly authority figure.

The next day the plan was to head west for Bardsey Sound - the subject of dire warnings in the pilot books - then north to Holyhead on the north west corner of Anglesey, a trip of about 58 miles. I left Pwllheli as late as possible on the ebb with the intention of sailing very slowly at first to be at Bardsey at slack water and take the tide through the sound.

The forecast was as benign as it could be and I motorsailed westwards in a very gentle southerly, past the fleet of forty three Dragons. An hour later, even as the Coastguard Manny was announcing on the VHF that the breeze was: "Variable, becoming south west, force three or less", the wind was blowing consistently at twenty to twenty four knots from the sodding north. Under the lee of the Llŷn Peninsula this made for a nice fast reach, but when I turned through Bardsey Sound with three knots of tide under me, a force six on the nose with wind over tide would be a nightmare. Bollocks.

I decided to speed up and stem the last of the contrary tide past Bardsey at least to avoid the wind over tide. This strategy worked. With two knots of tide against me it was slow progress but the sea was flat. Past Bardsey I headed due north into the teeth of a force five. As the tide turned a short chop was thrown up and I had to motorsail off the wind to maintain progress. Even so the larger waves stopped Zoph in her tracks. This was all very annoying. We are all used to complaining about the inaccuracies of weather forecasts, but the Met Office is usually very good at getting the wind direction right and this was the second of four passages in which they had got it wrong by 180 degrees.

We battered on with two reefs in the main and a reefed jib and me huddled under the spray hood, which is the closest Zoph has to a doghouse. After about 7.30 the wind dropped a bit, the waves fell away and we had over three knots of tide with us as we rounded South Stack. But the violent swirls and eddies were against us past North Stack as we turned east to Holyhead. This large ferry port is unattractive and the approach along the coast can be dodgy in the strong tides that swirl round the corner of Anglesey. It is however a large bit of water fully protected behind a huge causeway, with a load of yacht club moorings and a big marina.

Holyhead also had another of my elderly relatives, Uncle John, my Dad's octogenarian brother. He had a flat there and kept an old Hallberg Rassy on a club mooring. When I had phoned him up to say that I would be visiting he was utterly mortified that he was going to be away. I reassured him that I'd see him again soon but he was so passionately upset that he wasn't going to be there to meet me that I felt quite guilty that I'd not phoned sooner. Anyway I motored past his boat to the marina, tying up in the twilight at 9.45. That phone call was the last time I would ever speak to my Uncle John.

The Scouse Celts

I was still feeling guilty nine hours later as I left Holyhead for Peel on what used to be called, in less enlightened, more misogynistic days, the Isle of Man. On all but the oldest and most sexist of charts the Isle of Man is of course now called the Isle of Person. You may also know that Peel used to be called Ravenscroft until it changed its name in the 1960s in order to sound trendier on the radio. My sixty two mile passage was another which would span two tides. I let the tide carry us north east towards Morecambe Bay, then when it turned about five hours later we had gone far enough north to pick up a north west flowing tide which swept us towards the Isle of Person. For once my tide strategy worked perfectly and motorsailing at about five knots through the water we averaged 6.1 knots over the bottom for the passage.

The weather was fine and I didn't need to cower in the doghouse this time. Not literally anyway. It was however July 14th and I was condemned to the doghouse figuratively. It was Anna's 50th birthday and I had done absolutely nothing about it, protesting lamely the difficulty of finding precious jewels and other priceless birthday offerings in the wilds of the Celtic Fringe.

The only thing that disturbed our gentle curve was having to change course to avoid a fast ferry heading from Belfast to Liverpool round the bottom of the island. I'd just noticed that there was a legend on the chartplotter which said "See lower zoom for details". Since it means 'higher zooms' I zoomed in. It said the same thing. I zoomed in again. And again. "Beware high speed craft" was written on the chart. I looked up and there was a dirty great high speed ferry bearing down on me. Though I changed course a little I was actually the stand on vessel and it was reassuring to see on the AIS that it did actually change course by ten degrees or so to avoid me. Some of these things are going so fast that the only way of avoiding a collision is for them to change course. You are going too slow to make a difference.

I saw three or four other yachts once I'd rounded the Calf of Person and was heading towards Peel. I called Peel Harbour on the radio. A little later I heard "Station calling Douglas Harbour, this is Douglas Harbour". It took me quite a while to work out that they were talking to me, even though I clearly hadn't called Douglas Harbour.

The cognoscenti know that outside office hours Douglas Harbour staff, on the other side of the island, operate Peel Harbour Radio and the footbridge that has to be raised to enter, with the help of the hundreds of CCTV cameras that line its banks. Since the Peel Harbour employees are, by and large, a lazy bunch who just sit in their office looking at the telly, in truth this makes little real difference. What's important to the mariner is what harbour you are operating, not whose office you are sitting in while you are doing it, as I felt it my duty to communicate when I got the chance. If, however, you aren't in the know and entirely the wrong harbour comes on the radio telling you what time you can enter, you'd be forgiven for ignoring them. The manny in Douglas was somewhat irritated and patronising to any visiting yachtsmen who dared to assume they were talking to Peel harbour.

The wind increased so we sailed the last half hour or so and at about 5.30pm I picked up one of the four rather uncomfortable waiting moorings in the bay off Peel harbour. Rather worryingly, each of the big yellow buoys is marked in big black capital letters "MOOR AT OWN RISK". I did so. There was already a rib on one mooring, a small yacht on another and a larger Danish yacht on the other, so I had the last one. Soon another Danish yacht arrived and rafted up on the first one on the mooring - very chummy. It was low tide and Peel Harbour, formerly drying, now has an automatically operated raising sill which only lowers to let you in a couple of hours before high water at springs, one hour at neaps. Though this happens automatically someone also has to press a button to operate a raising footbridge over the sill.

Waiting outside Peel Harbour

This creates two problems in visiting Peel. The ideal time to leave the harbour heading north for the North Channel would be fairly early on a rising tide. In this case that would be about seven the following morning. Otherwise you are likely to run into a strong contrary tide up the North Channel. Since you can't get out except near high tide, this would have meant an uncomfortable night on the mooring or bumping about on the outer harbour wall, being buzzed by large trawlers all night.

The other problem is that the Harbourmaster - be he in Peel or Douglas - has absolutely no control over the opening of the sill. Incredibly, it just rises and lowers when the tide reaches a certain level and they just need to guess when that will be. On the ebb you are encouraged to enter at speed in case the sill suddenly rises. Apparently this has resulted in the keel being removed from at least one fishing boat who's skipper was over-enthusiastic about getting into the harbour on a falling tide. It seems nearly unbelievable that there isn't a manual override enabling the powers that be to postpone the raising for a few seconds to avoid the destruction of harbour traffic, but apparently there isn't.

Sixty years of going backwards in 50ft yacht design: A Nicholson from 1959 and a Moody, circa 2009

I prevaricated for some time about whether to enter the harbour for a couple of days or stay outside and press on the following morning. In favour of pressing on was the fact that the forecast was for a south westerly the following day, followed by a couple of days of northerlies, including a near gale in 48 hours time. In favour of staying were several factors. Firstly I had done 340 miles over the last seven days and though the majority of the passages had been easy I was still a bit knackered from doing this solo. I fancied a day without going anywhere. Secondly the forecast, though south westerly, was for a force five to six. This would be fine except that my preferred destination, Portpatrick, was rumoured to be rubbish to enter in strong south westerlies. Thirdly and crucially, I had never actually set foot on the Isle of Person even though this was the second time I'd been there.

The first time was when I was eight, at the end of the only passage race I've ever taken part in. Accompanying my uncle John, of Holyhead fame, my father and cousin, we'd raced a folkboat from the Mersey to Douglas overnight. My role in the crew was as a small amount of ballast. After a rough night and having had a slightly queasy stomach further irritated by Uncle John's scarcely cooked streaky bacon butties with extra lard, I'd been looking forward to getting ashore. As we floated about in the outer harbour I could see the ice cream shops and other attractions on the quay. But the wind was strong and must have been from the north, because the adults decided it was too rough to stay and go ashore. The ice cream was practically snatched from my youthful grasp as we turned back out to sea and I watched the Isle of Person disappearing astern as we ran all the way to Holyhead, rolling in the swell.

Now, on my second visit, my mind was made up, I was getting that ice cream at last. I inflated the dinghy - the first time I'd used it since Glandore, over a fortnight before - and rowed ashore. The absolute calm of the enclosed inner harbour, lined by pubs, further confirmed my decision. One pilot book showed Peel Harbour as drying. A two year old pilot showed the sill maintaining water levels, but no pontoons. Now the harbour is filled with posh new pontoons opened in 2009 by a local nabob. There's plenty of space for visitors and decent facilities. It's cheap enough by the day, as well, but annoyingly there is no weekly rate. You just pay the same amount for each day stayed, which makes it rather expensive for longer stays.

The new marina in Peel, with Zoph roughly in the middle

From the seafront I saw another yacht arrive, a Beneteau 32. Incredulously I watched as it attempted, in the moderate rolly swell, to raft up next to Zoph on her mooring. Was this standard practice round here? Rafting up on moorings without permission when boats are pitching and rolling about like mad? Eventually the Beneteau gave up and went and anchored. Challenging the skipper about this later it appeared he was in fact something of a novice who, seeing the two Danish chums rafted up, had assumed that this dubious practice was standard.

I rowed back to Zoph and waited until the sill and the footbridge opened at 9.45pm, joining the scramble to enter the harbour. In the end this proved a considerable tactical error and I didn't finally manage to leave it again for another twelve days.

Peel is in fact a beautiful little town, with a motley collection of organic streets and rows of brightly painted terraced houses tumbling down to the harbour. On the sea front are signs of slightly better times as the row of fine four storey Victorian holiday flats looks, on closer inspection, somewhat jaded and run down. All in all however, it's a pleasant, low key, old fashioned town that, with its butchers, bakers, drapers, grocers etc and relative lack of big name chain stores, does feel that it's stuck, in a pleasant sort of way, in about the early 1970s.

I was really unsure what to expect of the Isle of Person. I confess to a bias against all our tax havens for the rich. It has always seemed to me outrageous that the likes of Jersey and Guernsey can claim all the benefits and none of the obligations of UK citizenship. A denizen of the Isle of Person can, for example, live and work anywhere in the UK or the rest of the EU for as long as they wish. Someone from the rest of the UK and Europe, on the other hand, needs a work permit for the island. In the Channel Islands it's even worse and you can't even live there without permission, which you can get if you are as rich as Croesus. These are entirely unequal and inequitable relationships which would not be tolerated if these poxy little islands were much larger.

Given the propensity of the English in particular to rampage roughshod over all parts of the British Isles, not to say the world, it might seem surprising that this little island retains such a degree of autonomy. Every other part of the Celtic Fringe - including even, at one time, the Garlic Fringe - has been conquered by the English at some time or other. Yet the Manx have remained able to sit out in the middle of the Irish Sea, in sight of the English Lake District, thumbing their noses at empire. But this shouldn't come as a surprise. A central tenet of English - and later British - policy towards the rest of the world has been to conquer it. Another central tenet is that the rich must be allowed to keep all their money. Together these two principles have resulted in little pockets of land remaining where the normal rules don't apply and the rich aren't threatened by the democratic process.

Sadly this never actually happened

The streets of Peel

The Scottish Government should have a go at this. Designate some farty little bit of Scotland - Mull or Unst or Burntisland - as a haven with a flat rate of income tax of 10p in the pound then persuade Bill Gates to take up residence and watch the money roll in. One problem would be the fact that the super-rich never pay any tax anyway. The other problem would be that politicians would have to abandon all morality and sense of fairness and act purely amorally out of naked greed, which is surely unthinkable, isn't it?

My preconceptions about the Isle of Person were that I should expect to see lots of motorbikes, cats with no tails, people with three legs and all manner of minor celebs in huge Mediterranean style villas behind twelve foot high electrified security gates. I knew there were some celebs. I believe, for example that the arch anti-eco campaigner and geriatric adolescent Jeremy Clarkson 'lives' on the Isle of Person - or at least has an address there - where he perpetrates a massive tax double whammy. Paid millions in tax-payers money by the Government-owned BBC, that same Government then allows him to pay no tax by pretending to live in a tax haven. No wonder he gets annoyed when public sector workers complain at being swindled out of their pensions. Don't they know that they are snatching public sector money from the clutches of Clarkson, who needs more millions to secure his empire against the hordes of the unwashed? They really should bugger off and starve to death.

I did see a lot of motorbikes. They were mostly ridden by bald, overweight men in their late 50s wearing, under their snazzy leathers, tee shirts with legends such as "Live Fast and Die Young" stretched obscenely over their huge paunches. They were all, they believed, having fantastic outlaw adventures on the open road, having travelled from Manchester, got the ferry over from Heysham and ridden the island's lanes at exactly the speed limit. Apparently the hotel rooms on the Isle of Person all have magic mirrors in them. Whoever looks in them, what they see staring back is a youthful James Dean.

There was less evidence of cats with no tails, men with three legs or even, to be honest, Mediterranean style mansions.

With strong northerlies forecast I settled in for a couple of days. Another of my preconceptions was that a haven for the rich which needs to import everything would be expensive. Nothing could be further from the truth. The Island is filled with pubs selling lots of different local beers for as little - if you choose the rougher pubs - as £2.26 a pint. This was a very pleasant contrast to Ireland. The only really expensive thing was telephone calls. Annoyingly all the phone companies have chosen to count this little speck in the Irish Sea as a separate, foreign country and they charge accordingly.

The mean streets of Peel

Like the west of Ireland, several of the pubs in Peel had diddledee folk music jamming sessions which placed it very firmly in the Celtic Fringe. It was odd to hear this, however, almost exclusively in a Scouse accent on an island where very few people still speak the Manx language. It's not just the recent immigrants who speak Scouse. A sort of slightly toned down, gentle Liverpool accent is the dominant voice of even the twelfth generation locals. For centuries immigration has been mainly from Liverpool and Ireland. Liverpool of course has a long history of Irish immigration. I wondered if it was just coincidence that a basically Celtic population which had left Ireland for Liverpool then left Liverpool for the Isle of Person should find themselves, two hundred years later, playing basically Celtic music in Manx pubs. Who does this tradition belong to? The Manx, the Irish, the Scouse or the wider Gaelic world?

Another of my preconceptions was that Pool harbour would be filled with the super-yachts of the rich. Although there were a number of expensive things which looked like they never got used, the general mix was not dissimilar to Port Edgar, with yachts of different sizes and ages and a mix of racers and cruisers. Oddly there was certainly a lot more money in evidence floating about on the water in Pwllheli, impoverished Welsh town with little real economy, than in Peel, prosperous tax haven. It being Friday night the sailing club bar, which advertises itself as available to visiting sailors, was open and I nipped in for a pint. Its denizens were a friendly and inquisitive bunch and I soon got chatting to a few. Interestingly the most common accent after Scouse was Northern Irish. Sailors from Strangford Lough and Bangor seem to treat Peel as a local destination and several Irish folk keep their boats in Peel and commute at weekends. It's further evidence that the Isle of Person does rather sit at the fulcrum of the Celtic Fringe.

In the club I spoke to one couple who sail a 50ft ferro-cement ketch called *'Silver Duet'* out of Peel, where the bloke lives aboard all year. I casually asked them if they'd done any cruising this summer. "Well, it's funny you should ask" they said and proceeded to tell me the best sailing story I've heard all year.

On the evening of May 22nd 2011 Silver Duet left Peel heading for the hazards of the North Channel, the Mull of Kintyre and Gigha. Gales were forecast, increasing further the following day. These turned out to be the strongest winds that anyone can ever remember hitting the west of Scotland. The crew were the experienced skipper and his new girlfriend, who had never, ever, been sailing before.

With a following wind they made it to Gigha where they anchored in only a couple of metres of water, Silver Duet being too heavy for the visitors' moorings. With the wind from the south west they were at least in the lee of the shore. As the wind rose to hurricane force in the afternoon the boat was snatching badly at her anchor on its 25 metres of chain. The skipper went forward to put out more chain. This wasn't easy as the spray was blowing horizontally off the sea and it and the wind were making it hard to crawl forward. In order to put out more chain he released the windlass and either something broke on it or it slipped. The handle of the manual windlass snapped his upper arm in two. I quizzed his girlfriend on whether this was a fracture or a proper, serious break. Apparently the arm was dangling and flapping as if on a second elbow. This was no fracture but a proper snap, like well chopped firewood.

He made it back to the cabin and, apparently calmly, sent out a Mayday. It was way too rough to launch any boats so even though they were just yards from the shore a helicopter was sent out from the Clyde. According to its report, with a top speed of 145 knots it was able to make only thirty knots over the ground, such was the strength of the wind. Arriving on the scene the skipper was lifted off by the chopper, which must have been just as painful as breaking his arm.

It was at this point that their shiny new relationship, as well as the boat, nearly ended up on the rocks. The girlfriend, with no previous experience of sailing, left alone aboard a yacht in the worst storm in living memory, with winds topping 100 knots, was naturally expecting to be lifted off as well. But her caring partner, doubtless in great pain, from the throbbing chopper, tried to insist that she stay with the boat. "You can't leave, you have to stay and look after the yacht" he said. Incredulous, she declined in language not fit to be reproduced here and was herself taken off by the helicopter.

Three days later someone went over to fetch the unscathed boat and the skipper was subsequently asked to write a piece for Yachting Monthly about the experience. The relationship, grounded temporarily on the rocks by the skipper's prioritisation of boat over bird, was later refloated and patched up.

Seven weeks on the two of them were now planning their next cruise and having a laugh about it all. When I spoke to him, complete with a metal pin in his arm, he was worried about what to write for Yachting Monthly. Specifically, he had a problem with what to write under the heading 'lessons learned' - a standard part of the format of these stories.

The beach next to Peel Harbour

"I can't think what I could possibly have done differently" he said. "You should have stayed at home" I replied. "But the hurricane wasn't forecast". "They'd been forecasting a huge summer gale for nearly a week". "Yes but only a force nine. What else could I possibly have done?" "You should have stayed at home". "But we'd have been OK if it was only a force nine". "It was due to be at least a force nine up the North Channel and round the Mull of Kintyre, you should have stayed at home". "But it was only a force nine". "A force nine is up to 48 knots. You'd expect gusts two forces higher than that - up to sixty knots. You should have stayed at home". "I can't think what I could possibly have done differently" he said wistfully, staring off into space.

Having plenty of time I wandered the streets of Peel and wondered how things could be so cheap on an island that had to import everything. I wandered along the cliffs with the sea on one side and the pleasant pastoral fields and villages on the other. I took a bus to Douglas in search of billionaire's mansions to sneer at critically. It was slightly surreal to see red double decker buses on an island which feels in a way like a bit of the Hebrides. Heading to Douglas I was soon reminded that the population of Person is really quite large. But though the very English, suburban houses were substantial and prosperous looking, there was no real sign of obscene wealth.

Arriving in Douglas I realised why. The town is packed with banks and other financial organisations. These aren't the sort of banks that you used to pop into to get fifty quid out. These are banks that do 'Banking', with a capital 'B'. They look like mini bank head offices and their employees squirrel money away for their customers, moving it around from offshore account to offshore account. Behind each glass facade are the business addresses of hundreds of companies, none of whose directors have ever been there.

The super rich don't live on the Isle of Person - it's too cold and wet. They live in Bermuda. Their minions live in this tax haven looking after their theoretical addresses and moving their money about. They do very nicely out of it and drive Mercedes back to their suburban villas, but they don't employ teams of security thugs and live in walled estates.

The Isle of Person looks a reassuring, comfortable, old fashioned place in which to be well off, insulated from the politics and concerns and worries of the tax payers just over the sea and just over the horizon in every direction. Since they're theoretically Celts with a language, albeit a dead one, they even manage a little moral outrage at the supposed assault on their culture from outside and strive to sound hard done to. But they have difficulty maintaining any believable sincerity in their outrage, since it's blindingly obvious that they're doing quite nicely thank you.

It takes a peculiar type of ego to name a boat after yourself and I think *'Jolly Ollie'*, the tiny yacht next to Zoph on the pontoon in Peel, was the only example I'd ever seen. She was an eighteen foot bilge keeler plastered with sponsors' names and URLs, belonging to a young southern Englander called Ollie something-or-other. He's 'circumnavigating Britain' and one quick question was enough to establish that he went through the Caley Canal and was just doing the southern half. The 'Lowland Route'. To be fair, he did recognise that he was cheating and said that he hoped to trailer the boat up to Scotland and sail the northern bit next year. We shall see. His excuse for the short cut was that he had to be back in London in time to meet someone called 'Prince, William' who, the cognoscenti tell me, is one of the notorious Windsor family. Ollie was spending his time in Peel with his girlfriend, touting for sponsorship money.

One of the great things about cruising sailors is the unassuming way in which so many people, mostly old buffers, go about achieving amazing feats without the least fanfare. Contrast our self publicist Ollie, who was waiting for following winds of force four or less to motor from marina to marina, with the bloke on Silver Duet. The latter is entirely matter-of-fact about heading up the North Channel in a force nine. Or the couple who cruise from the south coast each year in a Vancouver. He's now eighty seven and blind, his wife, a couple of years younger, can luckily still see, so she does the navigation. Last time I met them they were heading for St Kilda. Or the old bloke I met in his nineties who sails a twenty foot junk rigged Colvic solo from the south of England, up the east coast to Shetland each year to visit his daughter, then sails back down the west coast. Or even the German bloke we met in Peel. He was sailing solo in a lightweight catamaran that amounted to little more than a racing dinghy. Each of the hulls had just enough room to lie down in and no more. He was heading north against the wind in an attempt to sail round Britain without using the Caley Canal and was doing so without any fanfare or sponsorship, just for something to do in his holidays.

Self-publicist 'Jolly Ollie' motored round half mainland UK

Meanwhile Ollie and his girlfriend are MacArthuring it up with their advertising stickers, and 'Support Ollie' web sites as he wanders the pontoons looking for a boat that's going the same way as him which he can chum along with as he motors in a flat clam to the next marina. OK he's not quite in the MacArthur league with the crying at will to a self-operated camera, but he's getting there.

The branding on Jolly Ollie makes it clear that he's getting the sponsorship and creating the hyperbole because he's recovered from leukaemia. Fair enough that's a rotten thing to get. It's a common reaction to recovering from cancer, it would seem, to want to sail round a significant part of Britain, for some unfathomable reason.

Ollie is doubtless described at being fantastically brave because he's had a cancer. This will be a contentious view but I've never really understood why it's supposed to be brave to have an illness. Early researchers into the causes of and cures for malaria injected themselves with the virus in order to test cures. Now that's brave. To give yourself a potentially deadly disease in order to help other people you don't even know takes selfless courage. To simply be told by a medic that you've got a condition and then undergo treatment is neither brave nor craven, it's just what happens. If you're shitting yourself throughout the process, that's not particularly brave. You are certainly to be sympathised with, but you are not necessarily brave.

This viewpoint may seem churlish but it has a serious intent. Giving the impression that only brave supermen can survive cancer is counterproductive and potentially damaging to the people being diagnosed. I was frequently annoyed that the American cyclist Lance 'The Boil' Armstrong was described as achieving an amazing feat because he could still ride his bike after recovering from bollock cancer. That's not amazing and it's not helping someone who's just been diagnosed with the condition to describe it as such. You ride a bike, you get bollock cancer, you think 'oh shit', you have the bollock snipped off, it hurts for a bit, you get some radiotherapy, you ride your bike again. You're not particularly brave, just a bit sore and knackered. So good for you Ollie, sailing and motoring round England, Wales and a bit of Scotland. I hope you enjoy your holiday. But don't expect a medal for it.

Person has plenty of twee industrial archaeology. This is the largest working waterwheel in the world

The northerly winds were refusing to abate and were forecast to continue for the forseeable future. Outside the shelter of the inner harbour conditions looked particularly crap in a north westerly and the buoys I had moored to on my arrival untenable. I decided therefore to leave Zoph and fly home to Edinburgh for a few days.

I returned nearly a week later with Anna, by train and ferry via Heysham. After a night showing Anna the fleshpots of Peel we headed out over the sill as it opened at six a.m. A Beneteau called *'Dansa'* who's skipper had expressed the intention of leaving showed no signs of life, but we were joined by a German Etap, which turned south outside the harbour. It was surprisingly rough just beyond the outer wall, with short, confused waves, but they settled into a more manageable pattern after a mile or so. With a force four still blowing from the north it was slow progress, but we battered into it with decreasing conviction.

The Coastguard came on the radio with a new forecast of north west force five and a moderate sea in the North Channel. Wimpily we decided that battering against twenty knots and wind over tide in the North Channel wasn't for us and turned back to Peel. I didn't fancy sitting outside the harbour on a mooring with the wind from the north, so when we were in range I radioed the harbour and was told that the sill should be down until about 8.30. We sped back under full main and jib and motor. As we did so, typically, three or four more boats came out of the harbour, but they all either turned south or headed west for Ireland. We made it over the sill at 8.15 and put the wasted two and a half hours and eleven miles down to experience. The buggers on the Beneteau still weren't out of bed, having decided to wait another day for a better forecast..

After breakfast we decided to explore the whole island by bus and train. Person has an old narrow gauge steam railway from its southern tip to Douglas, a horse drawn tram along the front at Douglas, an electric railway from Douglas to the north and another up to the Island's highest point, Snaefell, at just over 2000ft. We decided to cram in the whole touristic experience. A whistle-stop tour of practically every village on the island reveals that most are quite twee and have something to offer, but Peel is almost certainly the most attractive.

Douglas, aside from its banks, has a major shopping street and a long, long promenade looking windswept and past its best. The southern towns of Port St Mary and Castletown looked quite nice but Ramsey, at the north end, was frankly a bit of a dump. This came as something of a surprise, since I was given to understand that a lot of the folk with money lived at the north end. There were quite a few bit houses out in the country, but the town itself was definitely the low-light of Person.

A highlight was the top of Snaefell. Up there, at 2000ft on the middle of the land of the Scouse Celts, you really get a sense of how closely connected the bits of the Celtic Fringe are, once you forget about the motorway network and start travelling by sea. From there you can quite clearly see all the bits of Celtdom except Cornwall and the Garlic Fringe. You can see them clearly and unequivocally, close enough to touch, not just vaguely made out in the mist. Snowdonia, the Mountains of Mourne in Northern Ireland, the Wicklow Mountains and the Mull of Galloway are ranged out in front of you. The English Lake District is also clearly visible behind the almost impassable drying banks around Morecambe Bay. When the sea was the highway and the land mostly a barrier, all these parts of the Celtic Fringe must have been so familiar and the wilds beyond the English lakes - the boggy monotony of England - an unknown and unattractive land.

The next day, with a sense of déjà vu, we again left as soon as the sill dropped, this time at the slightly more civilised time of seven a.m. We were accompanied by Dansa which, having expressed the intention of heading for Portpatrick, soon changed course for Northern Ireland. Zoph was encumbered by several issues of 'Hello' and 'OK' magazine, which the wifey on Dansa had given to Anna as though she was doing her a favour. The vacuous faces of grinning celebs stared out at me as I resisted flinging the rags into the sea and tried to hold out for the next recycling facility.

We were followed out of Peel by a sixty foot sail training ketch with the less than glamorous name "Greater Manchester Council", also heading for Portpatrick but, with its deep draught, going slow to enter the small harbour at high tide. The wind was still blowing force three to four from the north north west but the sea was nothing like the washing machine of the previous day and the sun was out. Nothing bad can happen when there isn't a cloud in the sky.

To make best use of the tide and keep the wind at a manageable angle we motorsailed, steering a long way to port of our destination, towards Northern Ireland. After twenty five miles of this dog-leg into the middle of the North Channel we turned to starboard and the VMG instantly rose. With wind over tide it was choppy but at least we had the help of the tide. Eventually the wind dropped to a force two, the tide ran against us and the sea fell flat calm. Under these conditions we completed the forty four mile, nine and a half hour passage to Portpatrick, motored into the harbour and rafted up onto a wee Colvic motorsailer on the harbour wall. Zoph was back in Scotland having travelled about 1150 miles in the twenty nine day passages from Gigha, her last Scottish port of call.

Dunskey Castle near Portpatrick

Portpatrick

On Mill Pond

I'd never been to Portpatrick before. The small harbour is probably better known to Northern Irish than to Scottish sailors. It's a relatively short weekend hop over from Bangor and apparently a popular destination. On the other hand it's not particularly handy from any Scottish port and that corner of Scotland is something of a remote one for most of us by road. On the perfect summer's evening on which we visited it looked pretty idyllic. In the Irish model, the villagers have had the good sense to ensure that nearly all the buildings on the harbour side are pubs. I can't for the life of me understand why this has not been enforced by legislation elsewhere.

The harbour was perfectly quiet and calm and it was difficult to imagine the huge force of the waves which had fully demolished the massive Victorian quay and breakwater in the outer harbour. Over the years huge cut stone blocks weighing perhaps ten tonnes a piece had been dislodged from their places on the quay and flung fifty yards into the sea. The sight gave a clue as to why you'd want to take care entering Portpatrick in a strong south westerly.

As we walked the cliffs Zoph was joined in the harbour by a Contessa we'd seen in Peel and the romantically named 'Greater Manchester Council', which just squeezed into a reserved space on the wall. That evening, when we ate dinner outside one of the pubs watching the sunset, remains a reminder that we did actually have a summer in 2011, albeit a brief and fragmented one. There were perfect summer evenings.

Now that we were back in Scotland and Anna was on holiday we were in less hurry, but the next day we motorsailed in a perfect calm to Lamlash on Arran. On the way we passed close by the massive monolithic landmark of Ailsa Craig. Over on the mainland, fifteen miles away, there's a big road sign on the way into town that reads "Girvan, Home of Ailsa Craig". Happily the island wasn't aware of this and was still in the middle of the sea. The big ketch and the Contessa were anchored off Ailsa Craig in the perfect calm, but we motored on, skirting the shore slowly and as close as we dared. As we entered the outer Clyde it felt like I'd completed a series of transitions from one sea state to another. From open ocean, to sheltered ocean coast, to a big sea, to a smaller sheltered sea, to a large salty lake and finally to an enclosed millpond. Even the outer Clyde felt like a duck pond. Coming the other way, from the Forth Clyde Canal at Bowling, for example, the Clyde beyond Ailsa Craig feels like the open ocean.

In Lamlash Bay we picked up one of the last visitors' moorings, where we stayed for two nights as yet another wet depression blew through. The highlights of this, the third Arran I'd visited on the Celtic Fringe, were the catching of three mackerel and getting pissed in one of the piss-poor pubs with the campest gay couple you ever did meet. Surprisingly, they both worked in theatre in London. Who would have thought it. A camp gay couple working in theatre. Whatever next.

The following day we motorsailed then sailed round the bottom of Arran to Campbeltown. Now that we were in less hurry and the passages were shorter we could afford to sail in even very gentle breezes at much slower speeds, so the sail was a pleasant one. The pontoon at Campbeltown was busy and its occupants included a Vancouver 28, only the second Vancouver I'd seen since leaving Ardfern. The night was marred only by a refrigerated truck on the quay, which opted to run its generator all night in preference to plugging into the readily available mains electricity.

'Greater Manchester Council', winner of this year's crappest boat name competition

We had intended to sail round the Mull of Kintyre, but there is an annoying characteristic of that passage which often legislates against it. Clearly the best breeze for heading west round the Mull is an easterly or south easterly. The problem is that these are the very breezes that make the anchorage at Gigha untenable and the one at Craighouse uncomfortable. The forecast conditions were perfect for going round the Mull, but would be followed in the night by force six south easterlies, which would be utterly shite for sitting on a mooring at Gigha.

We therefore wimped out and sailed north to Loch Ranza, on the north west corner of Arran. After a very pleasant sail we picked up one of the last three available visitors' moorings and settled down for the night. The wind did indeed strengthen from the south east and brought with it a pile of really crap weather. We visited Loch Ranza's pub in the evening. This is probably Scotland's most expensive and meanest pub. Having paid him a fortune for a pint, the money-grabbing landlord wants to make a large charge for wifi. He also - get this - charges customers fifty pence to let them plug in a phone charger while they are drinking their overpriced booze. It is to be hoped that the miserable git goes out of business soon.

We stayed onboard on the mooring for most of the following day, letting the depression with its thirty knot gusts blow through. One highlight of the wait was a motor boat which picked up an adjacent mooring. One side of it had been painted up nicely. The other side was so knackered that I swear you could see gaping holes in the hull just above the water line. It was a miracle that it remained afloat.

Ailsa Craig

Another highlight was moron-filled yacht which couldn't pick up a mooring. It was, of course, a big Bavaria. In a force six and pissing down rain they made about six attempts to pick up a mooring and failed each time. Feeling sorry for them I jumped into the dinghy and rowed down to the mooring. On their next approach, once they got the idea, they were able to chuck me a line which I could pass through the mooring and hand back. Job done. But the conditions were bad and I was completely soaked by the exercise and knackered from rowing back to Zoph against the wind and waves. Nevertheless, back on board, I had a warm glow of satisfaction from my good Samaritan act and the Bavaria was now safe and snug on a mooring. I watched incredulously as, half an hour later, while I was trying to dry my soaking clothes on the charcoal stove, the bastard Bavarian ingrates dropped the hard-earned mooring and motored off out to sea in the lashing rain.

Towards evening the wind and rain subsided and we headed north up Loch Fyne under jib. As the wind died we motored. It was a Bank Holiday Sunday and we reckoned Tarbert would be rammed, so we headed for the new marina at Portavadie. As we entered the rectangular harbour and picked up one of the hundreds of empty pontoons off the massive motorway of main pontoon, it was absolutely pissing down with rain.

Portavadie is Britain's poshest marina, bar none. Practically empty aside from a few regulars, the building of it has been funded by a lunatic with an awful lot more money than sense. The harbour was built speculatively as a rig construction yard in the early days of North Sea oil. It was never used and the derelict facilities have now had a massive central pontoon and about two hundred finger pontoons installed. A row of posh modern flats has been built on shore and this block contains the bar and restaurant, as well as toilets, showers etc. The whole ensemble screams 'tax dodge'.

What was needed for passing yachtsmen was a portacabin selling beer. Instead there is a modern glass 'grand design' the size of Stanstead Airport, which must have cost many millions of pounds and could accommodate perhaps twelve people, sitting on sofas or at the bar. The bogs include a 'Family Bathroom' with a large bath. Tiling the walls and floor in natural stone must have cost at least as much as constructing an entire facilities block anywhere else. The gents even has proper, plug in hair driers and, I am led to believe, hair straighteners. The whole place is posh beyond belief.

Yet it's three quarters empty. By land it's a million miles from anywhere and by sea it's up a bit of a dead end. It seems to me extremely unlikely that the mad proprietor will ever make his money back, but good luck to him. With an eye for a bargain a couple of Port Edgar boats seem to have wound up berther here, including the Ronautica 33 'Robo' of my acquaint. One of the few visiting boats by the way, in what would become a recurring theme, was Dansa, the 'Hello' disgorging Beneteau from Peel.

Next day we motored to Ardrishaig and into Scotland's most expensive and difficult canal, the Crinan. A very cheery girl took £79 off us and we headed for the first lock. Unlike the Caley and the Forth-Clyde you have to operate nearly all the locks yourself. Of course the couple of locks that are operated by professionals are automated and involve the pressing of a button. Those that you have to operate yourself are manual and involve the strength of ten gorillas.

Anchored off Ailsa Craig

We could see right through the planking on this boat's port side, just above the waterline

We had just missed Dansa and another boat, which went through all the locks ahead of us. Though mob-handed they went incredibly slowly, leaving all the locks full, sometimes with the gates open. This meant that we - more specifically Anna - had to close the gates and do part of their job for them, as well as emptying every single bleedin' lock. The process took forever. As they pottered along ahead of us, obstructing our passage and making life difficult, they occasionally gave us a cheery wave.

We met Dansa once more, about a month later, in Troon marina on the Clyde. Zoph was back home in Port Ed and we were through there by car for other reasons. Cap'n Dansa, slowly heading back south for the winter, couldn't quite get his head round us being back on the Clyde. Travel at five knots by boat for long enough and you forget that people can zoom around at sixty miles an hour and cross the country just for the afternoon.

On the Crinan Canal the mood was not lightened by a grumpy bridge-keeper who, annoyed that his job involved the pressing up to four buttons a day, tried to force us to use his patented warping technique and, when I refused, opened some sluices rapidly enough to have Zoph careering all over the lock.

It was a long, slow day, but we still had hopes of making it to Crinan by evening, since the 'Skippers' Guide' clearly said that the canal operated until 5.30pm. At Dunardry Lock at 4.30 the sluice handles were missing and I phoned the canal office to enquire about this. Soon an operative arrived and explained that, though the contract I'd signed up to said the canal operated until 5.30, it really only opened until 4.30 because of staff cuts. With relish he encouraged me to complain about it. It seems the staff of British Waterways are operating a policy of being as obstructive as possible as a means of protesting against staffing cuts. Paradoxically, faced with the possibility of losing their jobs, they all bugger off home an hour early.

We spent a pleasant enough night marooned at Dunardry in company with a scruffy old plywood Uffa Fox Atalanta and a million midges. In the morning we headed for Crinan. Again it took forever to get through the remaining locks, since the folk responsible for levels in the canal had got it wrong and there was far too much water flooding into the canal at the top to be able to open any of the gates. It was around midday before we finally got out of the canal and motorsailed south in full sun for Craighouse. Though the forecast was for sun all day, after a couple of hours we got poor visibility, dreich and then rain. We also got three hours of contrary tide due to our late start from Crinan

Lochranza

Pointlessly assisting some clueless Bavarian ingrates who couldn't pick up a mooring

After a pleasant enough night on a mooring at Craighouse in company with several other boats, including another Vancouver 27, we motored out towards Gigha in the morning. We were accompanied, for some reason, by frantic waves from the couple on the stupidly named steel yacht, 'Happy', sitting on another mooring. In full sun and a flat calm on August 3rd we picked up a visitors' mooring at Gigha in very much the same conditions as when I'd left there on June 3rd. I suppose theoretically that completed my circumnavigation of Ireland. The log showed 1305 miles since I was last on Gigha.

Anna had never visited the island before so we did a whistle-stop tour of the gardens and other highlights. Back on board I had a quick swim. The sea temperature had finally reached fifteen degrees. That this was my sole dip of the year says something about the summer.

The afternoon flood would take us north so instead of staying the night we motorsailed off to Ardfern. The daftly named yacht 'Happy' was also at Ardfern and I discovered why they had been waving at us. Happy is Steve Kelvin's boat. Steve runs the boatyard at Grangemouth on the upper Forth. Zoph has been fixed a couple of times there and Steve is responsible for the embarrassing fact that Zoph's Windex is on back to front.

Steve told me he bought the boat in Germany when it was already called 'Happy'. I remarked to him and his wife that it's a particularly naff name, only made at all acceptable by the fact that it was named by a non-English speaker. Steve appeared to agree. I went on about it quite a lot more. Months later I was at Grangemouth helping to collect Ian Cameron's new boat, the Rival 38 *'Cherry Ripe'*. Whilst I was there Steve told me that his wife loves the name 'Happy'. In fact that was the only reason he was allowed to buy the boat. Sorry Steve's wife.

'Cherry Ripe', by the way, isn't a much better name for Ian's boat than Happy is for Steve's. As I'm sure you can guess, Cherry Ripe is painted bright... green. Yes, that's right, green. She is named, apparently, after a dreadful painting of a little girl by the Pre-Raphaelite Sir Kenny Everett Millais, painted using saccharin instead of oils.

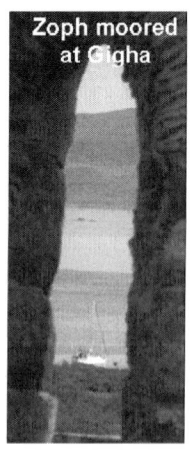

Zoph moored at Gigha

A small ship belonging to the Sea cadets was on the pontoon at Ardfern. In order to train these Sea Cadets it's apparently important that the ship operate its generators all night to provide heat and light for the poor darlings. It's also important, apparently, that rather than use the toilet facilities provided by the marina, the hundred or so boys and girls all poo on board, flushing the results directly out and creating a foul stench that pervades all the pontoons. I am unclear what the little dears will learn from this experience aboard a ship that looks like a miniature P&O ferry. Presumably it's just to teach them to develop thick skins and not give a crap about anyone else. For comfort and sanity we motored a mile or so to the quiet anchorage just along the road called 'the Lagoon' for the night.

In the morning, after picking up fuel and water at Ardfern, we sailed and motorsailed down Loch Craignish, caught the start of the west flowing tide through the Dorus Mhor and got up to five knots of tide with us north through the Sound of Luing. I often wonder what the sound of Luing is. I think it's a sustained middle C. We sailed up the Sound of Kerrera and took a pontoon at the busy marina on Kerrera.

We were doing our best to avoid the crush of West Highland Week. This annual event attracts hundreds of racy yachts of all sizes, each with a crew of twelve blokes with prodigious thirsts. It's basically an extended nautical piss-up in which expensive boats raft up eight deep in any conditions with little thought for their hulls or anyone else's boats or sleep patterns. Since the fleet was due in Oban after racing from Tobermory, the next morning we headed past Lismore and up the Sound of Mull. We bypassed the fleet, heading the opposite way under spinnakers, by taking a southerly route into the Sound. This had been recommended by the wifey who runs the marina as the best way of stemming the contrary tide and getting a back eddy. As it turned out she was completely wrong and we got a load more tide against us than other boats which just ploughed through the middle of the racing fleet to the north. We nipped into Loch Aline intending to anchor but instead took one of their brand new pontoons, installed two weeks before. A manny prowls the shore enthusiastically extracting too much money for a 27ft boat given that there's no facilities at all. 'Happy' and four other boats joined us.

Given that the racing fleet had now deserted it, we headed for Balamory the next day. The tide was with us and we had a gentle breeze so we sailed at 2.5 to 3.5 knots most of the way. Loads of boats were heading for Tobermory but none except for Zoph was sailing. This seems to be a west coast disease. Everyone is in a hurry to get somewhere by tea time and even though they're only going fifteen miles or so they motor there. We passed a lot of boats we recognised including a couple of Vancs and *'Northern Spirit'*, the superyacht which seemed to have been messing around the locality all summer. On the moorings in Balamory were a pile of boats we recognised from Port Edgar. There was a Vancouver 32 which used to live in Port Ed, our companion from the delivery trip in April, Solpieter and the motor-sailer *'Windsong'*. There seemed to have been a mass migration.

We decided against the bright city lights of Balamory and headed across to Loch Drumbuie. With a northerly forecast we anchored in the north east corner, next to yet another Vancouver. I went ashore for a walk and looked down on the loch as a stream of other boats came in and circled around Zoph looking for the best spot to anchor. As I rowed back to Zoph I saw that one of the new arrivals was *'Zanzara'*. This was a yacht once owned by my old Uncle John, of Holyhead fame. He had cruised extensively in her for years, including a trip out to St Kilda which he never tired of talking about. I wondered vaguely who was sailing her now.

Avoiding the West Highland Week fleet

"We've been invited aboard Zanzara for a drink" Anna said as I arrived. We rowed over and met Anna, Janice and Jenny from Port Ed. These were folk we knew and had sailed with a number of times in the past. Zanzara was now Anna's parents' boat. I had even met Anna's mum in Madeira when I was sailing to the start of the ARC on Equinox. I knew they had a small yacht but not, obviously, that it had an Edge family connection.

In the morning we sailed back down the Sound of Mull. With a following breeze we poled out the jib and goose-winged nearly all the way. The day was marred by the fact that it started pissing down for the last two hours before we arrived on the pontoon. There were yet more Vancouvers. Including Zoph there were four Vancs visiting Kerrera.

A Gigantic Whinge on the Celtic Fringe

109

Zoph in Loch Drumbuie

Swirly tides up the Sound of Luing

Yet another Vancouver

Two misinformed sailors

Now You Are Living In us JESUS

Treading Water

The migration from Port Edgar seemed to be continuing. The Ronautica *'Eurobo'* and the 44ft wooden long keeler *'Bosun'* were on nearby pontoons and I chatted to both skippers. The next morning Anna got the train home as her holidays were finished and she needed to get back to work to keep me in the style to which I had become accustomed. It wasn't bad timing actually. We'd had a pretty good spell of weather - by 2011 standards - which now looked set to break.

As the crap weather arrived I spent the next night in Kerrera then had a wee sail the next day up the coast of Lismore to Port Appin, where another visiting Vanc was moored, then back to Dunstaffnage to await the next depression sweeping through. To be honest I had begun to feel like I was just time wasting now. It was not yet the middle of August, but there was a sense that the holidays were over and I was just treading water. Like a kid who's been called in for his bed time and is just trying to eke a few more minutes out of a dying summer's evening.

At Dunstaffnage there were two more Vancs on moorings and one on a pontoon. Over the previous three days I had seen eleven Vancouvers. For the whole of the rest of the summer I had seen only one. The reason normally given for the numbers of Vancs on the west of Scotland is that the Vancouver is a tough, no nonsense cruiser built like a brick shithouse and ideally suited to difficult conditions and big seas. So why, then, are there so many on the west of Scotland which is, for the most part, Britain's easiest and most sheltered cruising ground? Far from being the wild and woolly place it's often thought to be, it's the one bit of Britain where there's always somewhere to go, where much of the water is sheltered from all directions and where a deep water all weather haven is never far away. Yet it's packed with uncompromising heavyweight cruisers.

The evening was enlivened by the antics of the crew of a brand new, big Northern Irish Jeanneau as, mob-handed and with someone ashore taking lines, they made a total arse of trying to come alongside a long outer pontoon with room for about four such boats. As so often happens, the skipper was presumably employing some fancy technique involving springs and motoring hard backwards and forwards. People read about these techniques in the sailing press and employ them in preference to getting a single line fixed in the right place, which in ninety nine out of a hundred situations is the right tactic. If you think you have to motor hard to get out of trouble you are probably doing something wrong.

Later, in the bar, the skipper was busy blaming the bloke ashore taking the lines, whose fault it clearly wasn't. He seemed to be saying that he'd only managed a couple of sails this year as it was too difficult to get off and on the pontoon. Astonishingly, yet quite commonly, the bloke had no fear of heading across the North Channel in a force six, yet was terrified of moving about in a marina.

The longer term forecast was for more crap weather - not big gales but lots of wet stuff - for the forseeable future. I phoned round a few places and found a mooring available for ten quid a day at Linnhe Marine, behind Shuna Island. Dunstaffnage was too expensive. The last straw there was that, whilst their website advertises free electricity, when you come to pay they demand money for connecting to it. Leaving the shysters behind I sailed off into the gloom for Shuna.

The millpond cuts up a bit rough

The posh chap who runs the low key operation there is very chatty and friendly to yachties. He does have some rather feudal views about everyone else however and seeks to chase people off 'his' beach, presumably having little knowledge of how access legislation has moved on in the last thousand years or so. He was jolly nice to me though, organising a lift ashore and even driving me to Ballachulish, from where I got the bus to Edinburgh, abandoning Zoph to look after herself for a few days as depression after depression swept the country.

Five days later when I returned it looked like it hadn't stopped raining for so much as a minute. But the forecast was for an improvement so I dropped the mooring and headed across the short distance to the visitors' moorings at Kingairloch in Loch a' Choire. Here the skies cleared and I spent a pleasant evening characterised by the presence of self-deluding lunatics. The first of these was on a boat on the adjacent mooring. This was a pleasant looking small ketch - I think it may be a Nantucket Clipper - with dodgers stretching half the length of the boat with the legend "Now You Are Living In us JESUS". The second self deluding nutter is the person who owns the estate.

Kingairloch is the site of the super-quarry which is exporting whole mountains to act as road aggregate for countries that don't have rocks, like Holland. This massive scar on the landscape is a one-off act of vandalism providing jobs for about three people that will see the land scarred for ever and whole mountains buried under Dutch tarmac. It's obviously making plenty of money for the estate and they are spending some of this by renovating some of the cottages they evicted people from 150 years ago and turning them into holiday cottages. There's also a new restaurant for the foody estate owner to run as a hobby a couple of days a week in the summer.

Kingairloch estate is run by a latter day Marie Antoinette

As of 2013 'Beware of Water' signs will be compulsory every 100 yards around all coasts

You can stay in the Old Gatehouse, where there are no gates, Pier Cottage, where the pier is derelict or The Old Post Office where, needless to say, you can't buy a stamp. Two nights a week you can have dinner in the Old Boathouse, where there's no boats. The whole ersatz setup, with a manufactured rural idyll deserted for ten months of the year and bankrolled by the massive wreckage of the quarry - just tastefully out of sight of the Laird's house but in everyone else's face - brings Marie Antoinette to mind. I half expected to see the wifey who runs the Old Boathouse wandering around in a massive frock with a bejewelled shepherd's crook.

That night I had one of my rare goes at fishing and caught one small mackerel. In a radical experiment I used a stainless vegetable steamer, a broken mandolin string and the charcoal stove on Zoph to smoke the fish. This was a resounding success and I'm willing to bet that there's not one 27ft yacht in a thousand on which there's a working smokery.

In the morning I sailed off the mooring in the very gentle breeze and headed past the surreally huge quarry towards Loch Aline. Though there was rarely more than eight knots of breeze I wasn't in a hurry so sailed all the way. Motoring southwards and overtaking me came a Tradewind 39 with the bizarre but familiar name *'Bimba'*. A bimba is, presumably, a female bimbo. So what sex is a bimbo? I'd last spoken to them the previous year in Campbeltown when we were taking Dave Punton and Neil McHugh's new boat *'Kittiwake'* from Bristol to the west coast. Before that I'd been aboard Bimba on South Uist and in Arisaig. Bimba stopped for a chat. They were just returning from a summer cruise to the Russian border with Norway, well above seventy degrees north and almost thirty east. This is way, way beyond the Lofoten Islands where I'd been with Zoph three years previously. They kindly offered dinner on board that night in Loch Aline. I say kindly, but they offered it aboard someone else's boat, which was to prove a tad embarrassing.

With three miles to go to Loch Aline the wind, fickle and variable all day, became a steady force four from the south west and I sailed into Loch Aline and right to the northern end, where I anchored. Dinner aboard a large catamaran, with the Bimba crew and a pair of liveaboards was very pleasant. The cat, though only 38ft long, was something of a three bedroomed flat with a living room and a dance floor. It was quite startling how much electrical kit they managed to run from a bank of twelve volt batteries. There seemed to be little concession to nautical living and no hardship on this floating suburban bungalow on which they wandered around, anchoring in a couple of feet of water off beaches.

By this time I was really just absorbing some of the relatively decent weather on offer before heading back into the Caley Canal and the next day I sailed even more slowly out of Loch Aline and back down the Sound of Mull. I was intending to stay to the west of Lismore, but then, at round about high water, I heard the following exchange on the VHF as a bloke with a Northern Irish accent came on channel sixteen.

"Clyde Coastguard this is yacht *'Tenacity'*. We've grounded on some rocks and the tide's ebbing. We don't appear to be holed but are worried we might be". "Can you describe your boat sir". "She's a blue Swan 56. A navy vessel flying a British Virgin Islands flag". "And what is your position sir". "We have just left Ardfern and are on rocks just off the southern end of Loch Craignish"... There was a long silence, then the Irish voice again... "Correction, we have just left Dunstaffnage and were heading up the Lynn of Lorne". Well no wonder he'd hit the bleedin' rocks. This was the skipper of a 56ft yacht, apparently a naval vessel, though this seems odd, who had

Linnhe Marine at Shuna

no idea where his boat was. He wasn't just a bit wrong, he was thirty miles out. Between where he thought he was and where he actually was is the Dorus Mhor, the Sound of Luing, Puilladobhrain, Kerrera, Oban and Dunstaffnage. No wonder they had run aground.

Obviously I just had to sail over and have a look at the casualty. I felt it my duty to be pointlessly nosey even though it was a long way off my intended course. By the time I arrived the Swan was indeed high and almost dry and the poor lifeboat crew were spending their day just drifting about nearby in case they might be required. Since there was no deep water anywhere near the Swan this seemed unlikely.

I headed on north past Port Appin and Shuna and picked up a somewhat uncomfortable, but free, mooring off the Holly Tree Hotel at Kintallen. The forecast was for near gales later the next day so I left at nine a.m. to get the first of the tide through the Corran narrows. At first it was breathless and a lovely calm sunny morning. The skipper of the ferry that scuttles back and forth at Corran was at the top of his game. Scuttler skippers are trained to leave just at the right time to cause maximum anxiety to passing yachts. Their aim is to make sure that you are the stand on vessel, then head straight for you just when you think you're going to get past before they leave the slipway. This one was bang on target. To paraphrase Blakey "I hate you Scuttler".

Loch a' Choire

Loch a'Choire

Livery

If taking the boat to the west coast for the summer is a delivery trip then the reverse, taking her back east, is presumably a livery trip.

We entered the sea lock with a wee Corribee crewed by two Gordonstoun schoolteachers. The biggest, most expensive looking gin palace you ever did see was at the top of Neptune's Staircase and, as such monstrosities are given to running their engines all night in a bid to rid the world of fossil fuel, we headed onwards to Gairlochy. Here the Gordonstoun teachers came aboard for a pint and to tell me about educating the thick offspring of the very posh.

The lock keepers gossiped about the gin palace. Apparently *'Kathleen Ann'* had just sat in the canal all summer. Someone chartered her and left the canal at Corpach, but then changed their minds and she had to be brought back into the canal. She's 129ft long, has a crew of six and can sleep as many as ten 'guests'. This is at least as poor use of space as on Northern Spirit. If you fancy hiring Kathleen Ann she's a snip at £125,000 a week. Yes, that's one hundred and twenty five thousand pounds a week. A day's hire is about what Zoph's worth. Apparently someone brought her to Fort Bill because he or she was looking for a house in the area and needed somewhere to stay whilst he or she was looking. The charterer's informative website where I found the price says "The Inner Hebrides are closer to Scotland... while the Outer Hebrides (are) about forty miles west of Scotland.... with lots of ferries running back and forth to Great Britain". Which is useful. How else would I have found out that the Hebrides are no longer part of Scotland, or even Great Britain?

Bimbo just back from the Norway/Russia border

Loch Aline

£125,000 a week to rent this massive caravan

The following morning - Saturday - Anna drove up from Edinbugrh to join me and we sailed down Loch Lochy. There was a fair old blow from the south west so we shot up the loch at between five and eight knots under just a jib. As we approached Laggan Locks we were down to a tiny scrap of reefed jib and still making five knots. There's a bumper-boat hire operation at Laggan Locks and Saturday afternoon is their big day for starting off through the locks, so I worried a little about their competence and the dangers posed to Zoph. I shouldn't have worried about them. I should have worried about my crew, with all her experience and RYA Incompetent Crew Certificate.

We had to wait for the lock so I motored round to windward and onto a pontoon which Zoph was blowing off slightly. Anna jumped off with a bow line and secured it to a forward cleat on the pontoon. I hopped off with a stern line. Secured to the pontoon Zoph blew gently away from it. Perfect. Except that Anna had omitted to tie the bleedin' line onto the boat. At all. So of course the bow blew off leaving a short length of line in the water and Zoph merrily sailed off the pontoon, attached only by the stern, with both of us stood on the pontoon. I managed to leap back aboard and deploy another line and no real damage was done, but I looked around me nervously. It is to be hoped that any watching crews embarking on the nearby bumper-boats were clueless enough not even to spot that this ridiculous performance wasn't deliberate.

We stopped for the night at Laggan and had a pleasant evening. We were invited aboard an LM30 from Sneck for a glass of red wine which Anna managed not to spill on the upholstery, followed by a pint in the pleasantly eccentric floating pub on a big old barge.

The following day we sailed slowly down Loch Oich, stopping for a late breakfast at the pleasant pontoon halfway down the north shore. Afterwards progress was slow as inevitably the next set of locks was closed for lunch, the lock keeper being tired and shagged out after having to press a button up to four times in the morning. Arriving at Fort Augustus at 2.15p.m. we joined the vast throng of bumper-boats and others waiting at the top of the cascade of locks. This was slightly fraught as there was every chance of being rammed by the loonies using far too much throttle to manoeuvre their unfamiliar charges.

It was made more fraught by the arrival up the locks of the naff converted CalMac ferry *'Lord of the Isles'*. We had to wait for three hours for Lord of the bloody Flies to be locked up. Apparently this stupid thing always gets priority in the locks. This despite the fact that they only pay the same amount per metre of length as everyone else. This massive ship that fills the locks and had the entire British Waterways staff dancing attendance all day pays less than four times the amount Zoph pays for a licence. For a while it looked like we weren't going to get down the locks that evening, but in the end we got our chance and tied up at the bottom, at the entrance to Loch Ness, at 6.15p.m.

Heading for the Corran Narrows

Our run of Caley Canal luck continued as we once again had a following breeze to sail up Loch Ness. We had a leisurely run up the loch and were passed by our chums in the LM with an unspellable Gaelic name and a very shiny big Dutch steel yacht called *'Boris'*. I'd seen Boris from about half a mile away a couple of days before and immediately announced that she looked like a Dutch yacht even though I couldn't see her flag. The Dutch typically have the most sturdy, solid, seaworthy, uncompromising, world-girdling yachts that could easily take you round Cape Horn. They then sail them round and round small freshwater ponds four feet deep. We were also passed by the huge, sleek sloop *'Bloodhound'*, heading back to Leith. We'd met the crew of Bloodhound in Kerrera. Built in 1936, she was 'owned' by Phil the Greek for a long while. She's now kept next to the Windsor's old dinghy *'Britannia'* in Leith Docks, where she sits and rots for most of the year. For two months every summer she gets out and this year had spent most of that time on a pontoon at Kerrera. What a waste.

We stopped for the night at Dochgarroch, where we were later passed by a bizarre charlatan. Heading south down the canal was a 32ft yacht from Liverpool absolutely covered in massive sponsorship stickers, urls and maps of Britain on which Scotland had been rendered as a tiny dot. They made the BBC maps look fair and objective. The yacht was crewed by two people, the youngish skipper and his girlfriend. Emblazoned on the side of the boat were the words 'Sailing Around Britain Single-Handed'. I commented as they passed on the fundamental inaccuracies in this statement and the bloke joked, of the girlfriend "Oh I just picked her up along the road". I pointed out that my primary concern was the fact that he was motoring through the middle of Britain, not going round it. He gestured casually, waving an arm to his right to indicate the two and a half million hectares on that side of the canal and said in a voice designed to carry to the ears of passing locals, "Oh that, that's not really part of Britain". What a Scouse tosser. I expect he stole the boat from someone.

It really is beyond me what these buggers hope to gain from their seedy wee deceptions. They are most unlikely to become rich and famous for their exploits like La MacArthur did. They aren't receiving personal payment for the voyage. So they must be hoping to gain a sense of fulfilment and achievement. But surely it's impossible to con yourself, even if you are able to con the rest of the world. Surely their sense of achievement will always be limited by what they actually achieved, not what they claimed to have achieved. Won't it?

Anna left that evening as I packed her back off to work. The next day I motored through to Seaport Marina, much of it in the company of Boris. This was a slow process. The lock keepers announced at Muirton locks that they had a technical problem with their VHF. It later transpired that the technical problem involved one of them dropping the radio into the canal. Arriving at eleven I was first told that they would lock me through at one p.m. Later I was told two p.m.. Then they started locking up another couple of boats so we had to wait until after 2.30. Since I was flying solo the two lock keepers said they would help with my lines. Unfortunately the two crew on Boris included the attractive, leggy blonde daughter of the skipper. As I handled the helm and bow and stern line on Zoph and tried to fend her off the lock walls, the Dutch girl tried to fend off the lock keepers. They were so desperate to ingratiate themselves with her that at times all three of them - both lock keepers and the Dutch bint - were holding the same bow line.

At Seaport I was anxious to make sure that I locked out to sea the following morning at eight, when the canal started operating, to make the most of the ebb tide. The manny who calls everyone 'Manny'. Said 'Aye manny we'll lock you out at 8.30 manny OK manny have a nice night manny'. At my protestations he just kept repeating the same mantra as the canal staff continued their work to not-actually-the-rules.

I left the canal, went under the

Kessock Bridge and out into shallow Inverness Firth in the morning in company with a Hallberg Rassy 49. At first sight she appeared to be called *'Random Squiggle'* but on closer inspection the squiggle resolved itself as *'Mach 3'*. She had four burly Dutch blokes aboard and I think had just been bought on the Clyde at Kip. They seemed to be having tremendous difficulty keeping to the channel. Perhaps the Dutch get nautical vertigo when the depth gets greater than two metres, but they were dodging about all over the place, over drying mud flats on a falling tide. Luckily for them they didn't come to grief and eventually settled on something like a course and pulled ahead of Zoph and out of sight.

The Souters at the entrance to Cromarty Firth

Unfortunately the wind, forecast to go southerly, persisted from the east north east and increased to a full force four. With wind against tide this made for an unpleasant chop so instead of Whitehills, where I had been heading, I plumped for Lossiemouth. A bit of care needs to be taken on the approach to Lossie due to the extraordinarily small, near invisible lobster pot markers off the coast. In fact in anything more than a mirror calm there's little point in taking care, because you're not going to see them until you've run over them. Some appear to be small brown pill bottles of the kind you get from chemists with twenty tablets in them. It is to be hoped that they are attached to easily snappable bits of string.

The next day I made the relatively small hop to Whitehills, motorsailing with a very gentle southerly. As the breeze increased we sailed for a while and were joined by a couple of porpoises for a stretch. Again I had intended to go further, around Rattray Head to Peterhead, but with huge towering rainclouds on the horizon over Frazerburgh I Googled the Met Office Rainfall Radar and confirmed that it was pissing down at Rattray Head, so I nipped into Whitehills. What a wimp. On second thoughts, can porpoises stretch? They do look kind of rubbery but they've no legs to stretch. Perhaps I was just joined by a couple of porpoises for a short period.

Whitehills is the cosiest harbour on the Moray coast and its facilities are great. A whole bungalow is provided for the few visiting yachts with, as well as the usual bogs and showers, a microwave, book shelves, sofas, a kettle and central heating. Its only real drawbacks are the difficulty of entering the harbour in strong northerlies and the fact that, once inside, you are in a sort of deep concrete hole that you can't see out of.

I left the next morning at sunrise to get the tide round Rattray Head, motorsailing and sailing by turns as the wind fluctuated from zero to twelve knots from the south. From Frazerburgh onwards I had the tide with me as the sunny skies turned to looming, unforecast fog banks up ahead. These never got too thick however, the sea round Rattray Head wasn't too bad and I tied up in Peterhead Marina at 12.15, next to the unfortunately named wee bilge keeler with an old gadgie onboard, *'Shy Talk'*. Not a name I'd like to have to say on the radio.

Later Boris appeared, having come from Lossie and stemmed the tide around Rattray Head. Neither of us were going anywhere for a few days. As the coast of North America prepared for Hurricane Irene and they started talking about evacuating New York, a routine summer storm was forecast to lash the east coast of Scotland. Once again I headed off by bus to sit it out.

Whilst away I kept an eye on conditions on the interweb. On www.xcweather.co.uk the nearest observations to Peterhead are at Rosemarkie, just along the coast. On August 28th the first and most important story on BBC news reported that the evacuated city of New York had experienced winds of up to 68 knots. For the same time xcweather recorded an average wind speed of 65 knots at Rosemarkie. Unsurprisingly, this didn't even make the back pages in Peterhead, never mind the front pages in America.

Returning three days later I found Boris still there after a delightful holiday sojourn in Peterhead. They confirmed that Peterhead, whilst an excellent place to keep a boat for a few days, is a totally shite place to keep a person. Surprisingly, though the wind was forecast to go north west force five or so the next day, they had elected to stay one more day. We had been joined by a German X Yacht, the 44ft *'Xeniu'*. This was a club-owned yacht on a North Sea circuit with a series of crew changes. The skipper proudly told me that their 2.4m draught ruled out Stonehaven as a destination and that they were heading for Arbroath in the morning at 6.30. I said that, with Zoph's slower cruising speed, I'd never make it to Arbroath before the lock gates closed for the night, so I'd head for Stonehaven at about 7.30.

Staggering bleary eyed from my pit in the morning I was just in time to see

A Gigantic Whinge on the Celtic Fringe

Xenia, Warrior Princess, slip her lines and motor rapidly to the exit. Fifteen minutes later I heard the skipper on the radio telling Peterhead harbour, in perfect clipped English, that they weren't leaving after all. About thirty minutes later, having done my ablutions, had a caffeine fix, dozed a bit and got dressed, I poked my head out and saw Xenia, Warrior Princess, stopped dead at the entrance to the 'all tides' marina, stuck firmly on the sandy bottom at an hour before low water springs.

The marina manager arrived and the conversation on the radio continued, with the German speaking clearly in perfect English and the Harbourmaster talking broad Doric. Since the skipper was, understandably, having difficulty understanding what was said, the Harbourmaster spoke to the marina manager... "Aye aye ken fit richt the morn ye'll hae tae spik tae hum yersel ah'm feart yon gipe tumshie disnae spik gae gud English" he said, or words to that effect. Bloody foreigners eh? Come over here and can't speak the language.

The crew of Xenia Warrior Princess inflated the dinghy and put someone ashore with a line, with which they first tried to winch her off the sand then to heel her to reduce her draught. Back on the boat some numpty didn't tie the dinghy on properly and soon it floated off across the marina, leaving them stranded aboard with the tide still ebbing and most of the bottom of the boat now showing above water.

After a suitable delay for more caffeine Zoph sprang into action with a dramatic dinghy rescue. I left the pontoon and poked the bow in to the rocks where the dinghy had ended up, getting a line on it and towing it back to Xenia. Though they were suitably grateful their gratitude was probably tempered by annoyance and jealousy as, with them firmly aground Zoph, with a metre less draught, slipped past her and out to sea.

Two days later, In Port Edgar, I saw Xenia's skipper again. He was pacing the 'D' pontoon waving a chart and a copy of Reed's Almanac, both of which claimed that Port Ed was an all tides marina with a minimum depth of 2.5m. Meanwhile Xenia was high and dry, this time at least alongside a pontoon. Though he was demanding more water depth in a somewhat Germanic way, I had a lot of sympathy with him. If it says all tides it bloody well should be all tides. Change the depth or change the information. Anyway, I then got a prize of six bottles of German beer for having rescued the dinghy. Not bad for five minutes work.

Sailing south from Peterhead with fifteen to twenty knots from the north west I started out under full sail, but put in one reef then two as the wind increased. I'd left at low water as recommended by the marina manny, whose advice differed from that published in the pilot. He was absolutely adamant that he was right and the book was wrong. He wasn't. I had a strong tide against me for two hours and should have stayed in bed longer.

A few miles north of Aberdeen a sail appeared over the horizon. Some chums from Port Edgar, Charlie Hussey and Mary Watson, had acquired a 'new' boat, a wooden cutter built in the 1930s called *'Mat Ali'*. They were due to be sailing her round to the west coast and I wondered if the sail might be them. In fact it was a 40ft Beneteau. But the next boat was *'Matalan'*, sailing close hauled up the coast under staysail and double reefed main. I phoned Mary and we had a brief chat. They'd sailed from Port Ed overnight and subsequently went from Peterhead to Inverness in one passage, but there were three of them aboard.

Later the wind died a bit and I shook out my reefs for the sail to Stonehaven, going all the way under sail on a nice efficient reach. I've been in Stonehaven about six or seven times before and always mostly enjoyed it. It's a pictureskew village with a couple of good pubs on the front and though untenable in strong easterlies, ought to have been fine after the offshore winds we'd had for the past few days.

This time I wasn't looking forward to it however. The previous year I'd been in with Dave Punton and Ian Macaroon on Dave's old boat *'Merlin'*. As usual we'd tied up on the inner part of the east wall and gone to the pub. From the pub window we saw a fishing boat called *'Dalwhinnie'*. An odd name for a boat as Dalwhinnie is probably the place in Scotland furthest from the nearest fish. Cap'n Dalwhinnie was busy untying Merlin's lines and apparently casting her adrift. We rushed to her rescue and retied her to the much more dodgy outer end of the wall. "There's no yachts allowed here", said Cap'n Dalwhinnie. I protested that I'd been in several times in the past and always tied up there. "No you haven't, I've never seen you" replied the unfeasibly cocksure angler.

So this time I was wary. At first I tied to the dodgy outer end of the wall and went to find the Harbourmaster, who was

Charlie Hussey and Mary Watson's new boat 'Matalan'

neither in nor answering his landline or mobile. It soon became obvious this bit of wall was untenable. The scend was sending Zoph backwards and forwards, snatching at the ropes and scratching her topsides. The very high tides meant that her fender board - necessary in the conditions - could have caught under a protruding concrete lip as the tide rose, possibly causing considerable damage.

I enquired of some fishermen on a lobster creel boat, who this time were helpful and directed me to the north wall, next to the offshore training school ribs. Of course as soon as I was properly secured there, another fisherman came over from another lobbo-boat. This was a young lad in overalls and a rorty black car with go-faster holes punched in the exhaust. "I hate to be the bearer of bad news" he said in an incongruously posh English accent. So with the help of other fishermen I rafted up on another fishing boat, where I passed the night with Zoph rubbing up and down his hull uncomfortably. The harbourmaster continued to make himself conspicuous by his absence.

I decided, on principle, that I wasn't going to pay the high price demanded by Stonehaven harbour for this berth. It was a crap berth which was likely to result in damage to the boat, where I couldn't leave her unattended for more than an hour and where I had to be ready to leave at a moment's notice should the fisherman who's boat I was tied to come back. To cap it all I had no key to the bogs and none of the facilities expected in a sensible port. After a short visit to the pub, severely truncated by the unutterable drivel being spouted, very loudly, by a drug-addled young hippy at the bar, who was driving half the customers away, I spent a night of interrupted sleep on board. From 2.30 pm to midnight there had been no sign of the Harbour Master.

As I was untying the lines the following morning at six, right on cue the Harbourmaster finally turned up. "Morning, you owe me money" he said. "Well, no, I'm afraid I don't" I replied, quite pleased with myself for not caving in to authority as I usually would. He immediately, without further discussion, stomped off in high dudgeon muttering about phoning up all the other harbours for a hundred miles around. I shouted after him that I was happy to give him my name and address so that the Council, who own the harbour, could send me a bill and I could explain why I wasn't going to pay it. "I don't want your name and address, I want money!" He shouted without turning round.

I was determined not to be seen as just doing a runner, so I phoned him on his mobile and explained why I wasn't paying. He protested that he'd had to go to the dentist and that was why he'd not been there all day. In all probability realising that he might get in trouble for skiving off all afternoon, he eventually muttered that we should forget about it.

Later I had a quick squint online at Aberdeenshire Council's charges for visitors to Stonehaven. I also had a look around elsewhere at marina charges. Stonehaven want an incredible twenty squid a night. For a 27ft boat like Zoph this makes Stonehaven more expensive than any marina in Scotland except

Largs, Troon and Ardrossan, which are just marginally dearer. For a 24ft boat Stonehaven is more expensive than any marina in Scotland. In all marinas, of course, you get pontoons, proper shelter, electricity (often free), water, toilets, showers, laundry, often wifi, sometimes ice making facilities, chandlery etc.

At Stonehaven you get... nothing. Not even the peace of mind that your boat is OK for the night. There is a public toilet, locked at night, to which berth holders are supposed to get a key, but in the absence of the Harbourmaster you can't even get into the public bog. Whilst I'm happy to leave Zoph in the care of a marina for a week or two, I am almost certain that if I left her in Stonehaven unattended for an afternoon and she was damaged, I would not be insured. The insurers would assert - rightly - that I had irresponsibly left her in an unsafe place. Imagine a marina where you have to set an anchor watch ... and it's the most expensive place to berth in Scotland.

Surreally, not everyone has to pay twenty quid a night. Anyone with a boat less than 3.1m long gets a fantastic, knock-down rate fifteen quid a night. Yes, that's right. Fifteen pounds for a boat, as long as it's less than ten feet long. It seems clear that Aberdeenshire Council, true to their dour, miserable, penny-pinching North East reputation, just don't want bloody yachts.

Bidding the Harbourmaster a cheery good-day I motorsailed and sailed south for four hours against the tide in fourteen to twenty knots of wind. Then the breeze died and came back very gently from the south east. Wanting to make Port Ed that evening I'm afraid I motored quite hard and though we had tide with us for a few hours on balance there seemed to be more of it against us. However three hours at seven knots with the tide took us round Fife Ness and past Anstruther, after which the wind died completely.

After 5.30 p.m. the tide turned against us but I think I minimised its effect by passing south of Inchkeith and Inchmickery. When you're sailing for the day out of Port Edgar Inchkeith, about nine miles away, seems like quite a major hike. It's an adventurous trip into foreign waters. Arriving back after sailing more than 2000 miles it feels like your back yard. Though I must say the last few miles, plugging against the worst of a spring ebb, were slow. At about 9.30pm on the last day of August, in the dark, we slipped under the bridges and tied up at Port Ed on berth D22, the same berth I'd stopped paying for four months earlier, nobody having used it in the meantime.

As I approached the berth Anna lit the end of the pontoon with her mobile phone so that I could find it in the dark. This really was a sign of summer drawing to a close. For most of my trip around the Celtic Fringe it would have been perfectly light at 9.30 in the evening. Now September was a couple of hours away and autumn just round the corner.

Back though the Forth bridges

Postscript

Since leaving Port Edgar Zoph had done a total of 2225 miles in 432 travelling hours. Of that Anna had sailed with me for 585 miles, Fiona Harrison for 277 miles and I'd done 1363 miles solo. It had been a mixed, staccato cruise of many parts but an interesting one during which I'd seen most of the major bits of the Celtic Fringe.

I'd sailed seas varying from proper ocean to mill pond and as Anna drove me back home to Edinburgh I wondered about next year. Could I be arsed with big rolly oceans and Iberia? Should I take the wimp's route to the madding crowds of the Med through the French canals?

Or maybe I should have a go at bobbing to the Baltic. Watch this space, if you can be bothered.

Oh, by the way, it was George Orwell. The famous Blair driving the posh Grand Banks onto the fuel berth at Ardfern, that is. Orwell's real name was Eric Blair and his son can presumably fuel his wee ship for another few miles any time anyone says 'Big Brother' or 'Room 101' out loud.

This is one of four books so far describing Zophiel's cruises.

"Skagerrak and Back: Zophiel's Two Summer Cruises in 2007" is the first one and is a relatively short account of a North Sea circuit.

"Floating Low to Lofoten" describes her trip from Edinburgh north to the Norwegian arctic and back in 2008.

"A Gigantic Whinge on the Celtic Fringe: A Total and Complete Circumnavigation of Ireland and Britain by the Slightly Truncated Irish Route" is, if you can get past the misleading title, just about a trip around Ireland in 2011.

"Bobbing to the Baltic" is the tale of her 2012 trip along much the same route as described in Griff Rhys Jones' book 'To the Baltic with Bob', but with a pile more photos and descriptions of a lot more good places to stop.

I have also written two books about my travels – without Zophiel – in parts of Asia, Africa and Central America little frequented by Europeans. They are entitled *"Travels with my Runt"* and *"The Front of Beyond"*.

There's more sailing tales at **http://www.edge.me.uk/Sailinghome.htm**, where you will also find the colour photos contained in these volumes.

Printed in Great Britain
by Amazon.co.uk, Ltd.,
Marston Gate.